24 SONGS MENDELSSOHN

Felix Mendelssohn and Fanny Mendelssohn Hensel

ORIGINALLY CREDITED TO FELIX MENDELSSOHN AS 12 GESÄNGE, OPUS 8, AND 12 LIEDER, OPUS 9

John Glenn Paton, editor

Copyright © MCMXCII by Alfred Publishing Co., Inc.
16380 Roscoe Blvd., P.O. Box 10003, Van Nuys, CA 91410-0003
Cover painting: A watercolor by Felix Mendelssohn.
Staatsbibliothek Preußischer Kulturbesitz, Mendelssohn-Archiv, Berlin.

TABLE OF CONTENTS

PREFACE

When a Berlin publisher brought out *Zwölf Gesänge* (Twelve Songs), Opus 8, in 1827, only one composer's name appeared on the cover. The fact that three of the songs were the work of a second, unnamed composer remained a family secret. The acknowledged composer was the 18-year-old Felix Mendelssohn, the secret one was his 21-year-old sister, Fanny Mendelssohn.

Three years later the same thing happened again with *Zwölf Lieder* (Twelve Songs), Opus 9, ostensibly by Felix Mendelssohn. Three of the songs were composed by his sister, who was by then the newly-married Fanny Hensel.

Both Fanny and Felix died in 1847, and in the 1870s Felix's complete works were published in a multivolume series. Fanny's six songs were included, and a footnote to the table of contents acknowledged her authorship. But her name still did not appear with her songs.

This edition rectifies an injustice done to Fanny Hensel, although it must be said that she compliantly accepted her family's decision not to publicize her remarkable talent. It was only near the end of her life that her husband, Wilhelm Hensel, urged her to share her music openly with the public.

The Mendelssohn Family

Fanny and Felix Mendelssohn were born into a stimulating and inspiring family environment.

The Mendelssohn name was made internationally famous by Fanny's and Felix's grandfather, the philosopher Moses Mendelssohn (1729–1786). Moses had a frail, hunchbacked body, but a remarkable mind, coupled with great personal charm and humor. Rising from complete poverty, he was able, as a silk merchant, to support his wife and six children and to entertain the frequent visitors who sought him out for his wis-dom. Moses was the first Jew who wrote books in German and the first German who translated the first five books of the Bible directly from Hebrew. In a time when most Jews were not accorded civil rights or citizenship, Moses' intellect brought him universal respect. He was often heralded by those who supported full civil rights for the Jewish population.

Moses' second son, Abraham Mendelssohn (1776–1835), went to Paris to learn banking, but there he fell in love with a young visitor from Berlin, Lea Solomon. Her parents insisted that the young couple return to Germany, and so they settled in Hamburg.

Fanny [fani] was born on November 14, 1805, and named for Lea's favorite aunt. Felix [feːlɪks] was born on February 3, 1809. He received a Latin name, which means "happy."

Fanny, Felix and their baby sister Rebecca were still small when the family relocated in Berlin because of the unsettled political conditions of the Napoleonic wars. Abraham's banking business prospered, and a fourth child, Paul, was born. In 1816 Abraham, who believed that the outward form of religion is unimportant, had his children baptized as Christians and Lutherans. Felix, especially, became a devout Christian. He also insisted on keeping the Jewish name Mendelssohn, against the advice of others.

Lea Mendelssohn, who had studied with a pupil of J. S. Bach, gave her children their first piano lessons. Family members recalled that in their early years the children only played the piano when Lea was sitting beside them with her needlework.

Zelter and Goethe

In 1819 Fanny and Felix began music theory lessons with Karl Friedrich Zelter (1758–1832), who was a musical descendent of J. S. Bach. Abraham Mendelssohn had known Zelter since the 1790s.

On his way to Paris in 1797, Abraham stopped in Frankfurt where he met the famous poet Goethe. Upon learning that Goethe admired Zelter's songs, Abraham urged Zelter to travel to Weimar and make Goethe's acquaintance. Abraham's advice led to the meeting and life-long friendship of Zelter and Goethe. It is said that Zelter was the only friend with whom Goethe used the intimate pronoun *Du*.

Zelter and the other leading composers of Berlin believed that the best songs are like folk songs: simple melodies with simple accompaniments, and strophic in form (that is, with the same music repeated for each stanza of text). Goethe approved because the texts of such songs could be sung clearly and understood easily; he did not care for the complex songs of composers such as Mozart and Beethoven. When Zelter taught Fanny and Felix about songwriting, he naturally stressed the superiority of strophic songs over any others.

In 1821 Zelter traveled to Weimar for two weeks to visit Goethe. He took 12-year-old Felix with him; Goethe was charmed, and every day the boy played Bach fugues for the old poet. Felix did not forget to mention his sister; Frau von Goethe sang some of Fanny's songs and Goethe penned a little poem to her.

In 1822 the whole family visited Goethe in Weimar. Felix and Fanny played more Bach fugues for Goethe, who again approved Fanny's musical settings of his poems.

The Mendelssohn Home

Meanwhile, despite the outward tranquillity of the Mendelssohn home life, Fanny must have undergone great emotional stress. Early in 1821 Fanny and Felix viewed an exhibition of paintings by the talented Wilhelm Hensel. Hensel was 21, Fanny was 15; they fell in love almost at first sight. Lea was adamant:

Hensel was to go to Rome, where he had a scholarship to study painting, and he was not to write to Fanny. Hensel obeyed; Fanny and Hensel kept their engagement secret through a separation of six years. Hensel drew portraits of all the Mendelssohns from memory and slyly sent them to Lea. She softened to the point of allowing him to write to her, and Fanny heard the letters read aloud.

These years were a rich and stimulating time for Fanny and Felix. Berlin was the capital of the Kingdom of Prussia and the seat of a major university. Leading intellectuals who lived in or visited Berlin often found their way to the Mendelssohn home.

Sunday concerts at home with invited audiences were frequent events. Often professional musicians were hired to play Fanny's and Felix's new compositions. Fanny wrote many songs, claiming she did not have a gift for working out longer compositions. Felix wrote increasingly larger works which included: chamber music, symphonies, an opera and the brilliant *Overture to A Midsummer Night's Dream*.

The Songs

Zwölf Gesänge, Op. 8, were published by Schlesinger in the early months of 1827, appearing in two *Hefte* (booklets) of six songs each. About this time Felix entered the University of Berlin. Fanny was leading a domestic life, busy with her music and proud of the fact that her gifted brother still relied on her judgment in musical questions.

At long last Hensel came back from Rome. Fanny's engagement to him was announced in January 1829 and the wedding was planned for October 1829. In the meantime, Felix made his first visit to England. His return home was delayed by an injury in a traffic accident and he missed Fanny's wedding.

Zwölf Lieder, Op. 9, were submitted

to Schlesinger for publication on February 21, 1830. (There is no distinction in meaning between *Gesänge* and *Lieder.)* The songs were issued in two Hefte. The first, songs 1–6, was subtitled *Der Jüngling* (The Boy) and the second, songs 7–12, was subtitled *Das Mädchen* (The Girl).

Thomas Stoner's dissertation on the songs suggests an interesting performance possibility. If two singers perform the songs alternately from the two booklets, in the order 1-7-2-8-3-9, etc., the resulting sequence outlines a sentimental story of young love, separation, and death.

With the publication of Opus 9, we leave the two composers at a happy time in their lives. Fanny was a devoted wife, soon to be a mother; she valued these roles more highly than her calling as a composer. Felix was looking ahead to his career as a conductor and composer.

Later Generations

The Mendelssohn songs were often undervalued by later critics, who saw them as, among other things, conventional, sentimental and undistinguished. They were often condemned as products of a Biedermeier mentality (see the notes to *Abendlied*) by critics who expected art to challenge society in a revolutionary way. Such was not the style of anyone in the Mendelssohn family.

Obviously, the songs in Opus 8 are youthful works, some of which show Zelter's influence, which strongly emphasized simplicity and strophic form. Fanny and Felix knew the works of Beethoven, but they had little exposure to the revolutionary songs of Schubert.

The influence of the new Romanticism is seen in the exuberant personal expression of Fanny's songs. Her *Heimweh* bursts with feeling that is scarcely under control. Most of Felix's songs seem more restrained *(Abendlied),* or energetic but impersonal *(Im Grünen).* But it may be that Romanticism influenced his choice of texts from the remote past *(Maienlied)* or unconventional societal roles *(Hexenlied).*

The songs of Opus 9 represent a great stride in the direction of Felix's personal expression. In addition to the possibility that Opus 9 was meant to be sung in the manner of a song cycle, there is the peculiarity that the poets (perhaps even Uhland, who was a famous Swabian poet) were personally known to Fanny and Felix. This implies a desire on their parts to deal with the most advanced ideas known to them.

In evaluating the lieder, one should remember that they were meant primarily to be sung at home by amateur singers. Songs were occasionally performed in concerts with mixed programs, but no one had ever given a recital consisting exclusively of songs.

It would be a mistake to compare these songs to the lieder of Clara and Robert Schumann, whose famous songs were composed 10 years later, in 1840. Their songs, written under Felix's influence, benefited greatly from the new piano style developed by Robert Schumann in 23 opus numbers of piano music.

No matter how the Mendelssohn reputation varied in the intervening years, performers will find warmth, grace, clarity and balance in these songs.

ABOUT THIS EDITION

The musical text given here is based on Schlesinger editions preserved in the Mendelssohn Archive, which is housed in the Staatsbibliothek Stiftung preußischer Kulturbesitz (National Library Foundation of Prussian Cultural Possessions) in Berlin. These were examined and copied in July 1991. It is assumed that Fanny and Felix corrected these publications, which therefore represent their wishes better than any manuscripts that may survive.

All other currently available editions are based on the complete works, edited by Julius Rietz (Leipzig: Breitkopf and Härtel, 1874–77). Rietz was a friend of the Mendelssohns and a capable musician, but he apparently made editorial choices that are difficult to justify. For instance, wherever the Schlesinger edition had an acciaccatura with a slash through the stem, Rietz changed it to a cue-sized 16th note, a more old-fashioned style of notation. Compared with Rietz's edition, the first editions have many dynamic markings in different places, and they have far fewer phrasing and articulation markings. In some cases, Rietz's recommendations represent improvements in consistency and logic. Some of these have been retained, but printed in gray.

Two customs of German music publishers have been followed here: (1) the initial letter of a line of poetry is not capitalized in a song text; and (2) ß is replaced with *ss*. Spelling has been modernized in a few cases.

Each poem is presented along with a phonetic transcription and a direct translation of each individual word. The poem's background and source are given, with elucidation of unusual German expressions. Unique features of the music are noted, along with special points that affect performance.

At the foot of each music page is a further translation of the text in natural English word order; this may be used for recital program notes.

Grateful acknowledgment is due to my wife, Joan Thompson, who participated fully in our research work in Berlin and lovingly supports all of my work.

As always, I am grateful to the research libraries I have used, to their staff members and the governments that support them. My warm thanks go to Iris and Morty Manus of Alfred Publishing Co., to Robert Melyar and Linda Lusk, who had special responsibility for this volume, and to the many helpful professionals at Alfred.

John Glenn Paton
Los Angeles

RECOMMENDED LITERATURE

- *The Mendelssohns: Three Generations of Genius,* by Herbert Kupferberg. (An entertaining chronicle of the family from Moses Mendelssohn through the later generations to about 1950.) New York: Charles Scribner's Sons, 1972.

- *Mendelssohn: A New Image of the Composer and His Age,* by Eric Werner. (The most complete biography of Felix, including the issue of anti-Semitism and its influence on his career.) New York: Free Press of Glencoe, 1963.

- *Mendelssohn's Published Songs, by* Thomas Stoner. (A richly detailed and insightful Ph.D. dissertation.) Ann Arbor: University Microfilms, 1972.

- "The Lieder of Fanny Mendelssohn Hensel," by Marcia J. Citron, *Musical Quarterly,* Fall, 1983.

- "Fanny Mendelssohn and Her Songs," by Lorraine Gorrell, *NATS Journal,* May/June 1986.

- *At the Piano With Felix and Fanny Mendelssohn,* edited by Maurice Hinson. (A carefully annotated collection of twelve piano pieces, including five previously unpublished works by Fanny.) Los Angeles: Alfred Publishing Co., Inc., 1988.

Queen Victoria of the United Kingdom and her husband, Prince Albert, were both avid amateur musicians and admirers of Felix Mendelssohn's music. This engraving from 1842 depicts Prince Albert playing the organ in Buckingham Palace in London, as the queen and Mendelssohn listen. Later during this informal private visit, Felix played the organ and Victoria and Albert sang.

On the piano in the queen's sitting room, Felix found a copy of his Opus 8 songs. When Felix asked to hear her sing, Victoria chose *Italien*. In a letter written to his mother, Felix said of the queen's singing, "It was really charming, and the last long G I have never heard better or purer or more natural from any amateur." When Victoria praised the song, Felix was forced to admit, with some embarrassment, that his sister had composed it.

After Prince Albert sang *Erntelied*, Felix improvised at the piano, combining the themes of the two songs and the organ piece that the Prince had played earlier.

MINNELIED
[mɪnnəliːt]

(Love Song)

hɔldər   klɪŋt   der   foːgəlzaŋ
1 Holder   klingt   der   Vogelsang,
Lovelier   sounds   the   bird-song

vɛn   di |ɛŋəlraenə
2 Wenn die Engelreine,
when   the   angel-pure-one,

di: maen juŋəs   hɛrts   bətsvaŋ
3 Die mein junges Herz bezwang,
who my   young heart overcame,

vandəlt   dʊrç   di   haenə
4 Wandelt   durch   die   Haine.
walks   through   the   grove.

røːtər   blyːən   taːl   ʊnt |ao
5 Röter   blühen Tal   und   Au',
Redder   bloom   valley and   meadow,

gryːnər   vɪrt   der   raːzən
6 Grüner   wird   der   Rasen,
greener   becomes the   grass-bed

vo: di   fɪŋər   maenər   frao
7 Wo   die Finger meiner   Frau
where   the   fingers of-my   wife

maeənbluːmən   laːzən
8 Maienblumen   lasen.
May-flowers   gathered.

oːnə   zi: ɪst |aləs   toːt
9 Ohne   sie   ist   alles   tot,
Without her   is   everything   dead;

vɛlk   zɪnt blyːt   ʊnt   krɔøtər
10 Welk   sind Blüt'   und   Kräuter,
withered   are   blossoms and   plants,

ʊnt   kaen fryːlɪŋs|aːbəntroːt
11 Und   kein   Frühlingsabendrot
and   no   spring-sunset

dʏŋkt mi:r   ʃøːn   ʊnt   haetər
12 Dünkt mir   schön   und   heiter.
seems   to-me beautiful   and   cheerful.

traotə   haesgəliːptə   frao
13 Traute, heißgeliebte Frau,
Dear,   hotly-loved   wife,

vɔləst   nɪmmər fliːən
14 Wollest   nimmer fliehen;
may-you-want   never   to-flee,

das   maen hɛrts   glaeç   diːzər |ao
15 Daß   mein   Herz, gleich dieser Au',
so-that my   heart, like   this   meadow,

møːg ɪn vɔnnə blyːən
16 Mög' in Wonne blühen!
may   in delight   bloom!

Ludewig Hölty (1748–1776)
[luːdəvɪç hœlti]

Poetic Background

"The whole world is fairer because of my wife's existence. May she remain always in my life!"

Hölty studied theology at the University of Göttingen, where he was a leader in a group of young poets. Unfortunately, he died early of tuberculosis, leaving a widow.

The poem is a rare one: a love song to the poet's wife. Schubert's setting of this poem is also strophic and in 6/8 meter. Brahms' setting, one of his finest songs, is through-composed.

According to *Brahms's Lieder* by Max Friedlaender (London: Oxford University Press, 1928), Hölty's original poem was written in 1773. All musical settings of it derive from an 1804 edition, extensively rewritten by Hölty's friend, J. H. Voß (who wrote other poems in Opus 8). Both Hölty's and Voß's versions are printed in *The Ring of Words* by Philip L. Miller (New York: Norton, 1973).

Line 3: *junges Herz* is Felix's change of text; Hölty and Voß wrote *Jünglingsherz* (youth's heart).

Line 13: *Traute, heißgeliebte,* is Felix's choice of words. Hölty wrote *Liebe, minnigliche* (dear, loving), and Voß wrote *Traute, minnigliche* (dear, loving).

Hölty's original poem had five four-line stanzas. Voß omitted the third stanza, leaving four stanzas; Mendelssohn combined them into two.

Interpretation

To begin his collection Felix chose a song that seems almost as simple as those of his teacher, Zelter. Even within this simplicity, Felix uses techniques that characterize all of his music.

The first two measures contain a melodic unit that is repeated at measures 5–6 and 13–14, but are harmonized differently each time. Also, a different path of movement leads away from each melodic unit, although each contains a rise and fall. (Brahms also liked to vary melodies in this way.)

At the final cadence (measures 16–17) the voice falls to the keynote, but the fall seems gently cushioned by the tender chords in the accompaniment, which only reaches the tonic chord a measure later. Altogether there are many hints that Felix will be a more interesting composer than his teacher.

Felix did not prescribe a crescendo in measures 3–7, but it seems natural, given the increasingly full accompaniment. The dynamic is again soft at measure 13. The crescendo in measure 15 needs to reach a peak on the first beat of measure 16 . In the complete edition *dim.* is printed directly over the note in measure 16, but that could mislead the performer into making an inappropriately sudden dynamic effect.

The second stanza stays in the happy mood of the first, only expressing a desire that that mood should go on forever. (Brahms, setting the same poem around 1875, set *Ohne sie ist alles tot* as a contrasting section with minor harmonies.) The augmented fourth leap (measures 11–12) seemed pointless in the first stanza, but the word *fliehen* justifies it.

Minnelied

Ludewig Hölty

Felix Mendelssohn
Opus 8, No. 1

Literal Translation:

1) Even the birds' songs sound lovelier when that pure angel who captured my youthful heart strolls through the grove.

2) The meadow flowers are brighter and the grass is greener where my wife's hands have gathered May flowers.

3) Without her everything is dead, the flowers and plants are withered, and no spring sunset seems beautiful and happy to me.

4) Dear, beloved wife, may you never leave me! so that my heart may bloom in delight like this meadow!

DAS HEIMWEH
[das hɑemveː]

(Homesickness)

vas ɪsts das miːr den |ɑːtəm hɛmmət
1 Was ist's, das mir den Atem hemmet
What is-it that to-me the breath inhibits

ʊnt zɛlpst den zɔøftsər ʊntərdrykt
2 Und selbst den Seufzer unterdrückt?
and even the sigh stifles,

das ʃteːts ɪn jeːdən veːk zɪç ʃtɛmmət
3 Das stets in jeden Weg sich stemmet
that always in every way [itself] opposes,

ʊnt zɪn ʊnt gaest miːr zoː fɛrrʏkt
4 Und Sinn und Geist mir so verrückt?
and mind and spirit of-me so makes-crazy?

ɛs ɪst das hɑemveː oː ʃmɛrtsənslaot
5 Es ist das Heimweh! O Schmerzenslaut!
It is [the] homesickness, o pain-sound!

viː klɪŋst ɪm |ɪnnərn miːr fɛrtraot
6 Wie klingst im Innern mir vertraut!
How you-sound in-the inside of-me familiar!

vas ɪsts das miːr den vɪllən raobət
7 Was ist's, das mir den Willen raubet,
What is-it that of-me the will robs,

tsu jeːdər taːt mɪç muːtloːs maxt
8 Zu jeder Tat mich mutlos macht?
for every deed me without-courage makes,

das miːr di fluːr zoː gryːn bəlaobət
9 Das mir die Flur, so grün belaubet,
that for-me the arable-land, so green leaved,

fɛrvandəlt ɪn gəfɛŋnɪsnaxt
10 Verwandelt in Gefängnisnacht?
transforms into prison-night?

ɛs ɪst das hɑemveː oː jammərtoːn
11 Es ist das Heimweh! O Jammerton!
It is [the] homesickness, o misery-tone!

viː laŋə tøːnst ɪm hɛrtsən ʃoːn
12 Wie lange tönst im Herzen schon!
How long you-have-sounded in-the heart already!

vas ɪsts das mɪç erʃtart ʊnt brɛnnət
13 Was ist's, das mich erstarrt und brennet
What is-it that me freezes and burns

ʊnt jeːdə frɔød ʊnt lʊst fɛrgɛlt
14 Und jede Freud' und Lust vergällt?
and every joy and desire spoils?

giːpt ɛs kaen vɔrt das diːzəs nɛnnət
15 Gibt es kein Wort, das dieses nennet,
Is there no word that this names,

giːpt ɛs kaen vɔrt ɪn diːzər vɛlt
16 Gibt es kein Wort in dieser Welt?
is there no word in this world?

ɛs ɪst das hɑemveː oː hɛrbəs veː
17 Es ist das Heimweh! O herbes Weh!
It is [the] homesickness, o bitter sorrow!

di hɑemaːt |ax ɪç nɪmmər zeː
18 Die Heimat, ach! ich nimmer seh!
The homeland, ah! I nevermore will-see!

Friederike Robert (1795–1832)
[friːdəriːkə roːbɛrt]

Poetic Background

"I suffer from the thought, how far I am from home!"

Many Romantic poems dealt with homesickness, an emotion that is primarily individual, not shared with others. Romantic poets tended to emphasize their individuality, their estrangement from society. In the early 1800s, however, many people left their homes unwillingly because of political unrest or because industrialization forced people from agricultural areas into large cities. Poems of this kind were popular in Germany, and folk songs about homesickness are sung to this day.

The poet, identified only as "Friederike" in the first edition, was born Friederike Braun in Böblingen, a suburb of Stuttgart. She and her husband, Ludwig Robert, were members of the Mendelssohns' social circle in Berlin.

Line 18: *Heimat* is translated "homeland", but the German concept is of the place where one grew up: a farm, a town, a valley, or whatever it may be.

Interpretation

Fanny has filled this song with marks of emphasis and dynamic contrast in a more impassioned Romantic style than any of Felix's songs in Opus 8. The fiery piano postlude is a forerunner of Robert Schumann's postludes.

In the first edition only the first stanza of the poem is printed with the music; the others are printed in poetic form following the music. It is not known whether Hensel would have expected a performer to sing all three stanzas.

Das Heimweh

Friederike Robert

Fanny Hensel
Opus 8, No. 2

Literal Translation:

1) What is it that stops my breath and even suppresses a sigh? What is it that hems me in and crazes my mind and spirit?
   It is homesickness, painful word! How well I know your sound within me!

2) What is it that robs me of my will and takes away my courage, that turns this fertile green countryside into a dark prison?
   It is homesickness, sound of misery! How long you have sounded in my heart already!

3) What is it that freezes and burns me and sours every joy and pleasure? Is there no word for this in all the world?
   It is homesickness, bitter pain! My home, alas, I shall never see again!

ITALIEN
[itaːli̯ən]

(Italy)

ʃøːnər   ʊnt ʃøːnər   ʃmʏkt zɪç der plaːn
1 **Schöner**   **und schöner**   **schmückt sich der Plan,**
More-beautiful and more-beautiful decks   itself the plain.

ʃmae̯çəlndə lʏftə veːən mɪç an
2 **Schmeichelnde Lüfte**   **wehen mich an;**
Coaxing   breezes blow me   along;

fɔrt aos der proːza lastən ʊnt myː
3 **Fort aus der Prosa Lasten und Müh,**
away from the prose's burdens and trouble

tsiː ɪç tsʊm landə der poeziː
4 **Zieh' ich zum**   **Lande der Poesie.**
aim I   toward-the land   of-the poesy.

gɔldnər di zɔnnə blaoər di lʊft
5 **Gold'ner**   **die Sonne, blauer die Luft,**
More-golden the sun,   bluer   the air,

gryːnər di gryːnə vʏrtsgər der dʊft
6 **Grüner**   **die Grüne, würz'ger der Duft!**
greener   the green, spicier the fragrance!

dɔrt an dem mae̯shalm ʃvɛllənt fɔn zaft
7 **Dort an dem Maishalm, schwellend von Saft,**
There by the corn-stalk, swelling with sap,

ʃtrɔøpt zɪç der aːloːə ʃtœrrɪʃə kraft
8 **Sträubt sich der Aloe störrische Kraft!**
struggles [itself] the aloe's obstinate strength!

oːlbaom tsyprɛsə blɔnt duː duː braon
9 **Oelbaum, Zypresse, blond du, du braun,**
Olive-tree, cypress, blond you, you brown,

nɪkt iːr viː tsiːrlɪçə gryːsəndə fraon
10 **Nickt ihr wie zierliche grüßende Frau'n?**
do-nod you like graceful, greeting ladies?

vas glɛntst ɪm laobə fʊnkəlnt viː gɔlt
11 **Was glänzt im**   **Laube, funkelnd wie Gold?**
What gleams in-the foliage, sparkling like gold?

ha pomərantsə bɪrkst duː dɪç hɔlt
12 **Ha, Pomeranze, birgst du dich**   **hold?**
Ah, pomegranate, hide you yourself charmingly?

trɔtsgər pozei̯dɔn vɛːrəst duː diːs
13 **Trotz'ger Poseidon! wärest du**   **dieß,**
Defiant Neptune, were you the-same-one

der ʊntən ʃɛrtst ʊnt mʊrməlt zoː zyːs
14 **Der unten scherzt und murmelt so süß?**
who below jokes   and murmurs so sweetly?

ʊnt diːs halp viːzə halp ɛːtər tsuː ʃaon
15 **Und dieß, halb Wiese,**   **halb Aether zu schau'n,**
And this, half meadow, half ether   to see,

ɛs vɛːr dɛs meːrəs fʊrçtbaːrəs graon
16 **Es wär' des Meeres furchtbares Grau'n?**
it was the sea's   fearsome horror?

hiːr vɪll ɪç voːnən gœtlɪçə duː
17 **Hier will ich wohnen! Göttliche**   **du,**
Here want I to-live! Divine-one you,

brɪŋst duː parteːnope voːgən tsuːr ruː
18 **Bringst du, Parthenope, Wogen zur**   **Ruh?**
Bring you, Parthenope, waves to   rest?

nuːn dɛn fɛrzuːx ɛs eːdən der lʊst
19 **Nun denn, versuch' es Eden der Lust,**
Now then, try   it, Eden of   delight,

eːbnə di voːgən aox diːzər brust
20 **Eb'ne die Wogen auch dieser Brust.**
smooth the waves   also of-this breast.

Franz Grillparzer (1791–1872)
[frants grɪlpartsər]

Poetic Background

"Arriving in Italy, I am delighted by the beauty of nature."

    Through the centuries many Germans have left the cloudy North to go to "sunny Italy." Goethe's travel writings caused literary persons to regard a visit to Italy as essential to their education. Grillparzer, an Austrian playwright and a friend of Beethoven, shared this enthusiasm. He may not have met the Berlin Mendelssohns, but he called on Fanny's aunt, Dorothea Mendelssohn Schlegel, at a time when both were in Rome.

    The poem was written in 1820. The original title was *Zwischen Gaeta und Capua* (Between Gaeta and Capua), two towns north of Naples.

    Line 9: *blond du, du braun* (blond you, you brown) refers to the light color of the olive tree and the dark color of the cypress. This contrast is a striking feature of the Italian landscape.

    Line 13: *Trotz'ger Poseidon* (Defiant Neptune) is the sea god, who seems defiant to Germans familiar with the North Sea. In the relatively quiet Mediterranean, he seems to "joke and murmur sweetly" (line 14). Notice that the second syllable of Poseidon does not follow German rules of pronunciation.

    Line 15: *Aether* (ether), in classical literature, is the blue sky. The sea here is smooth as a meadow and blue as the sky.

    Line 17: *Göttliche* (Divine one), having a feminine ending, refers to Parthenope.

    Line 18: *Parthenope* is the ancient name for the city of Naples, which is here addressed as the person Parthenope, a Siren or sea nymph. The Sirens sang so sweetly that seamen who heard them were lured to wreck their ships on rocks.

    Line 19: *Eden* is the Biblical garden of innocence, to

which the poet compares Italy.

The original poem had 13 four-line stanzas, each line half as long as those shown above. Fanny omitted stanzas 7–9 from the musical setting and shaped the remaining 10 short stanzas into 3 longer ones.

Interpretation

If the text were in Italian, this song could pass as a composition of Donizetti or early Verdi. It requires gusto, even in the third stanza with its mythological allusions. The grand climax (measure 40) makes perfect sense if one equates *Parthenope* with Naples, famous for its scenic bay. Imagine the excitement of emerging from a carriage to breathe the fresh sea air and see a spectacular view of the Bay of Naples.

An amusing story about this song comes from Felix's seventh trip to England in 1842. He was privileged to have a private visit with Queen Victoria and her husband, Prince Albert. The Queen remarked that she was fond of singing Felix's songs, and at Prince Albert's suggestion she agreed to sing one. She sang very well, according to Felix's account in a letter, but the song she selected was *Italien*. He wrote, "I was obliged to confess that Fanny had written the song (which I found very hard, but pride must have a fall)."

The appoggiaturas are printed as eighth notes; they must be performed as accented sixteenth notes. Appoggiaturas are explained in Vaccai's *Practical Method of Italian Singing*, published in 1833.

The tempo given in the first edition is Allegro vivace; in the complete works it was changed to Allegretto.

Italien

Franz Grillparzer

Fanny Hensel
Opus 8, No. 3

Literal Translation:

1) More and more beautiful is the countryside; enticing breezes blow toward me. Away from prosaic burdens and troubles! I am going to the land of poesy. The sun is more golden, the sky bluer, nature is greener, fragrances are spicier!

sie. Gold'-ner die Son - ne, blau- er die Luft, grü -ner die Grü - ne, würz'-ger der Duft!

(2.) Dort an dem Mais - halm, schwel-lend von Saft, sträubt sich der A- lo- e stör-ri- sche

Kraft! Oel-baum, Cy - pres - se, blond du, du braun, nickt ihr wie zier-li-che grü- ssen-de Frau'n? Was glänzt im

Lau - be, fun-kelnd wie Gold? Ha, Po-me- ran - ze, birgst du dich hold?

2) Next to the stalk of grain, swelling with sap, the rugged aloe plant struggles upward.
Pale olive tree and dark cypress, are you not nodding like lovely ladies in greeting?
What is shining there in the foliage, sparkling like gold? Ah, pomegranate, are you hiding there?

29 a tempo

(3.) Trotz'- ger Po - sei - don, wä- rest du dies, der un-ten scherzt _ und mur-melt so süss? Und dies, halb

a tempo

p

34 cresc. *f* *p* > molto cresc. - - - - - - - - - - - - - - -

Wie -se, halb Ae- ther zu schau'n, es wär des Mee-res furcht-ba-res Grau'n? Hier will ich woh- nen! Gött-li-che

f *p* cresc. - - - - - - - - - - - - *f*

> > >

39 *f* *f* ritard. molto a tempo *p* >

du, bringst du, Par - the-no-pe, Wo-gen zur Ruh? Nun dann ver - such'_ es, E- den der Lust, eb'-ne die

colla voce a tempo *p*

44 *sf* *p*

Wo - gen, die Wo - - - gen auch die - ser Brust.

p rit.

3) Defiant god of the North Sea, are you the same one who, down here, murmurs and plays so sweetly?
   Is this the same sea, smooth as a meadow, bright as the sky, that is fearsome in the north? Here I want to live!
   You divine Siren, Naples, can you calm the waves? Now try whether, in this delightful Eden, you can also calm my emotions!

ERNTELIED
[ɛrntəliːt]

(Harvest Song)

εs   ɪst aen ʃnɪtər   deːr haest   toːt
1 Es   ist ein Schnitter, der heißt   Tod,
There is a   reaper,   who is-called Death.

hat   gəvalt fɔm   høːçstən gɔt
2 Hat   Gewalt vom   höchsten Gott;
He-has power from-the highest God.

hɔøt   vɛtst er das mɛsər
3 Heut   wetzt er das Messer,
Today whets he the blade,

εs   ʃnaet   ʃoːn   fiːl bɛsər
4 Es   schneidt schon viel besser;
it   cuts   already much better.

balt vɪrt er draen ʃnaedən
5 Bald wird er drein schneiden,
Soon will he into-it cut;

viːr mʏsəns   nuːr laedən
6 Wir müssen's nur   leiden.
we   must-it only suffer.

hyːtə   dɪç   ʃøːns blyːməlaen
7 Hüte   dich,   schöns Blümelein!
Take-care of-yourself, pretty little-flower!

vas   hɔøt nɔx gryːn ʊnt frɪʃ   daːʃteːt
8 Was   heut noch grün und frisch dasteht,
What today still green and fresh there-stands,

vɪrt ʃoːn mɔrgən hɪnvɛkgəmɛːt
9 Wird schon morgen hinweggemäht:
will-be already tomorrow away mowed:

diː   ǀeːdlən nartsɪsən
10 Die edlen   Narzissen,
the stately daffodils,

di tsiːrdən der viːzən
11 Die Zierden   der Wiesen,
the adornments of-the meadows,

fiːl ʃøːn hyatsɪntən
12 Viel schön Hyacinthen,
many beautiful hyacinths,

di tʏrkɪʃən bɪndən
13,14 Die türkischen Binden. Hüte dich, etc.
the martagon lily.

fiːl hʊndərttaozənt ǀʊngətsɛːlt
15 Viel hunderttausend ungezählt,
Many hundred-thousand uncounted,

vas   nuːr ʊntər der zɪçəl fɛlt
16 Was   nur unter der Sichel fällt,
which only under the sickle fall,

iːr roːzən iːr liliən
17 Ihr Rosen, ihr Lilien,
you roses, you lilies,

ɔøç vɪrt er ǀaostɪlgən
18 Euch wird er austilgen,
you will he exterminate.

aox di kaezərkroːnən
19 Auch die Kaiserkronen
Even the crown-imperials

vɪrt er nɪçt fɛrʃoːnən
20,21 Wird er nicht verschonen. Hüte dich, etc.
will he not spare.

das hɪmməlfarbə ǀeːrənpraes
22 Das himmelfarbe Ehrenpreis,
The sky-colored   veronica,

di tʊlpaːnən gɛlp   ʊnt vaes
23 Die Tulpanen gelb   und weiß,
the tulips   yellow and white

di zɪlbərnən glɔkən
24 Die silbernen Glocken,
the silver   bells,

di gɔldənən floːkən
25 Die goldenen Flocken,
the yellow   centaurea—

zɛŋkt ǀaləs tsuːr ǀeːrdən
26 Senkt alles   zur   Erden;
sinks everything to-the earth.

vas vɪrt daraos veːrdən
27,28 Was wird daraus werden? Hüte dich, etc.
What will thereof become?

iːr hʏpʃ lavɛndəl rɔsmaraen
29 Ihr hübsch Lawendel, Rosmarein,
You pretty lavender, rosemarie,

iːr fiːlfarbgə røːzəlaen
30 Ihr vielfarb'ge Röselein,
you many-colored little-roses,

iːr ʃtɔltsə ʃveːrtliːliən
31 Ihr stolze Schwertlilien,
you proud irises,

iːr kraozə baziliən
32 Ihr krause Basilien,
you curly basils,

iːr tsarte vioːlən
33 Ihr zarte Violen,
you tender violas,

man vɪrt ɔøç balt hoːlən
34, 35 Man wird euch bald holen. Hüte dich, etc.
one will you soon come-for.

zoː veːrd ɪç fɛrzɛtsət
39 So werd' ich versetzet
so will I be-transplanted

trɔts toːt kɔm heːr ɪç fyrçt dɪç nɪt
36 Trotz! Tod, komm her, ich fürcht dich nit.
Defiance! Death, come here, I fear you not.

ɪn den hɪmlɪʃən gartən
40 In den himmlischen Garten,
into the heavenly garden,

trɔts ʃael daheːr ɪn aenəm ʃrɪt
37 Trotz, eil daher in einem Schritt.
Defiance! Hasten here in one step!

aof den ʃallə wiːr vartən
41 Auf den alle wir warten.
on which all we wait.

veːrd ɪç nuːr fɛrlɛtsət
38 Werd' ich nur verletzet,
If-be I only wounded,

frɔø dɪç duː ʃøːns blyːməlaen
42 Freu' dich, du schöns Blümelein!
Rejoice [yourself], you beautiful dear-flower!

from *Des Knaben Wunderhorn*
[dɛs knaːbən vʊndərhɔrn]

Poetic Background

"Everything must die, no matter how beautiful it is, but we will live on in Heaven." Many poems and pictures depict Death as a "grim reaper," but this mysterious poem uses horticultural language throughout.

Des Knaben Wunderhorn (The Boy's Magic Horn) is the imaginative title of a collection of verse that fostered the Romantics' curiosity about folk traditions and the remote past. The editors were Achim von Arnim and Clemens Brentano, and the first edition appeared in 1806–1808. (Stoner says that Brentano may have written part or all of this poem, but scholars do not agree about it.)

Felix used five song texts from *Des Knaben Wunderhorn*, and it later had a central significance in the works of Gustav Mahler.

Title: The first edition uses the archaic spelling *Aerntelied.*

Line 7: Who is *Blümelein* (little flower), to whom every seventh line is addressed? Is it a beloved person to whom you are singing? Or is it your own soul?

Line 23: *Tulpanen* is an obsolete word for tulips.

Line 33: *Violen* (violas) has a stress on [o] in this song, but on [i] in modern German.

Line 37: *Schritt* is *Schnitt* (cut) in the original poem.

Interpretation

Ordinarily, one would hesitate to sing five identical stanzas of a song, but Felix has written a haunting melody that can bear the repetitions. Each stanza ends with the dominant note being held by the voice while the piano completes the melody to the tonic. The resulting sense of incompleteness, even at the end of the song, creates a hypnotic fascination.

The quiet dynamic level of the first stanza must not necessarily continue through stanzas 2–5. A suggestion: Allow a crescendo in measures 5–15, with slightly more crescendo in each stanza, returning always to ***pp*** in measure 16.

The sixth stanza brings its own surprises, with a sudden change from mournful foreboding to resurrection faith. Felix's inspired addition of two measures (measures 36–37) creates a triumphant climax before the thoughtful closing.

In the first edition the music and words of the first stanza are printed together, the second through fifth stanzas are printed in poetic form, and the music and words of the sixth stanza are printed together.

Literal Translation:

1) There is a reaper named Death, who has power from God on high. Today he is sharpening his scythe; it already cuts well. Soon he will cut, and we must only suffer. Take care for yourself, pretty little flower!

2) What today is green and fresh will be mowed away tomorrow: the stately narcissus, glory of the meadow; beautiful hyacinths and lilies. Take care, little flower!

3) Uncounted hundreds of thousands fall under the sickle. You roses and lilies, he will exterminate you. Even crown-imperials he will not spare. Take care, little flower!

4) The blue veronica, the yellow and white tulips, silver bells and yellow centaurea: everything falls to earth. What will come of it? Take care, little flower!

5) You pretty lavender, rosemary, you little roses of all colors, you proud irises, curly basils, tender pansies: he will come for you soon. Take care, little flower!

Erntelied

Original key: A minor

Anonymous, from
Des Knaben Wunderhorn

Felix Mendelssohn
Opus 8, No. 4

Andante con moto

(1.) Es ist ein Schnit - ter, __ der heisst Tod, hat Ge - walt vom __ höch - sten
(2. Was heut noch) grün und __ frisch da - steht, wird schon mor - gen hin - weg ge -
(3. Viel hun - dert-) tau - send __ un - ge - zählt, was nur un - ter der Si - chel
(4. Das him - mel-) far - be __ Eh - ren - preis, die Tul - pa - nen __ gelb und
(5. Ihr hübsch La-) wen - del, __ Ros - ma - rein, ihr viel - farb' - ge __ Rö - se -

Gott; heut wetzt er das Mes - ser, es schneid't schon viel bes - ser; bald wird er drein schnei -
mäht: die ed - len Nar - cis - sen, die Zier - den der Wie - sen, viel schön' Hy - a - cin -
fällt. Ihr Ro - sen und Li - lien, euch wird er aus - til - gen, auch die Kai - ser - kro -
weiss, die sil - ber - nen Glo - cken, die gol - de - nen Flo - cken, senkt al - les zur Er -
lein, ihr stol - ze Schwert - li - lien, ihr krau - se Ba - si - lien, ihr zar - te Vi - o -

den, wir müs - sen's nur lei - den. Hü - te dich, schön's Blü - me - lein!
then, die tür - ki - schen Bin - den. Hü - te dich, schön's Blü - me - lein!
nen wird er nicht ver - scho - nen. Hü - te dich, schön's Blü - me - lein!
den; was wird da - raus wer - den? Hü - te dich, schön's Blü - me - lein!
len, man wird euch bald ho - len. Hü - te dich, schön's Blü - me - lein!

5

PILGERSPRUCH
[pɪlgərʃprux]

(Pilgrim Saying)

 las dɪç nuːr nɪçts nɪçt dɑ͜oərn
1 **Laß dich nur nichts nicht dauern**
Let for-you only nothing [not] make-sad

mɪt trɑ͜oərn
2 **Mit Trauern,**
In mourning;

zae ʃtɪllə
3 **Sei stille!**
be calm.

viː gɔt ɛs fyːkt
4 **Wie Gott es fügt,**
As God it ordains,

zoː zae fɛrgnyːkt
5 **So sei vergnügt**
so be pleased

mɑen vɪllə
6 **Mein Wille.**
my will.

vas vɪlt du: fiːl dɪç zɔrgən
7 **Was willt du viel dich sorgen**
Why want you much yourself to-worry

ɑof mɔrgən
8 **Auf morgen?**
about tomorrow?

der |ɑene
9 **Der Eine**
The One

ʃteːt |alləm fyːr
10 **Steht allem für,**
stands for-all in-favor;

der giːpt |ɑox diːr
11 **Der gibt auch dir**
He will-give also to-you

das dɑenə
12 **Das Deine.**
the yours.

zae nuːr ɪn |alləm hɑndəl
13 **Sei nur in allem Handel**
Be only in every transaction

oːn vɑndəl
14 **Ohn' Wandel,**
without changing;

steː fɛstə
15 **Steh' feste!**
stand firm!

vas gɔt bəʃlɔøst
16 **Was Gott beschleußt,**
What God decides,

das ɪst ʊnt hɑest
17 **Das ist und heißt**
that is and is-called

das bɛstə
18 **Das Beste.**
the best.

Paul Fleming (1609–1640)
[pɑol flɛmɪŋ]

Poetic Background
"Trust in God, who will make everything right in the end."

Fleming (or Flemming) was a physician, who spent five years of his short life in Russia and Persia.

Punctuation was little used in Fleming's time with the result that some lines of the poem may be translated in more than one way.

Line 7: *willt* is an archaic form of *willst* (want).

Line 7: *sorgen auf Morgen* (to worry about tomorrow); these words recall a saying of Jesus in Luther's translation of the Bible (Matthew 6:34).

Line 16: *beschleußt* is an archaic form of *beschließt* (decides).

Interpretation
The music expresses the first stanza beautifully, but in the second stanza the phrasing is awkward. Make it clear that *Der Eine* begins a new sentence by separating it carefully from the preceding sentence: *sorgen auf morgen?* (breath) *Der Eine...*, etc. Use a similar phrasing in the third stanza.

In the third stanza, where the phrases are extended, most singers will need a breath after *heißt* (measure 26). Notice that in repeating the last line of verse, Felix reversed the two verbs in order to have an [ɑ] vowel on the longer extended tone.

Pilgerspruch

Paul Fleming

Felix Mendelssohn
Opus 8, No. 5

Literal Translation:

1) Let nothing sadden you; in mourning, be calm. Whatever God ordains, may my will be content.

2) Why do you worry so much about tomorrow? The One who sustains all, will also sustain you.

3) In all your doings, do not waver; be firm! What God has decided is for the best.

Fanny Mendelssohn

 Fanny was regarded as a beauty by those fortunate enough to know her. This is one of many drawings by her future husband, Wilhelm Hensel (1794–1861). It is not dated, but it appears to show her at age 16, before Wilhelm went to study in Rome.

Hensel was charming and popular in society; he was also a wounded veteran of the wars against Napoleon. His poetic talent was encouraged by prominent poets. After his return from Rome he was named court painter of the kingdom of Prussia. After Fanny's sudden death in 1847, Hensel suffered long periods of depression and self-doubt. He died a heroic death in the act of saving a child who was in danger of being run over by a horse and carriage.

FRÜHLINGSLIED
[fry:lɪŋsli:t]

(Spring Song)

jɛtst kɔmt der fry:lɪŋ der hɪmməl ɪʃ blao
1 Jetzt kommt der Frühling, der Himmel isch blau,
Now comes the spring, the sky is blue

di ve:glə zɪn truˍkən di lyftə ge:n lao
2 Die Wegle sin trucken, die Lüfte geh'n lau.
the little-roads are dry, the breezes go mild.

jɛtst kɔmt der fry:lɪn di fø:glə ɪm valt
3 Jetzt kommt der Frühling, die Vögle im Wald
Now comes the spring, the birdies in-the wood

tsvɪˍtʃərn ʊnt lɔˍka i:rə vaˍeblə vo:l balt
4 Zwitschern und locka ihre Weible wol bald.
twitter and entice their little-females indeed soon.

jɛtst kɔmt der fry:lɪn di bɛ:m ʃlɑˍ:gə |aos
5 Jetzt kommt der Frühling, die Bähm' schlage aus,
Now comes the spring, the trees bud out

ʊn i: brɪŋ mae ʃɛtslə aen faˍegələʃtraos
6 Un i bring mei Schätzle ein Veigelestrauss.
and I bring my darling a violet-bunch.

Friederike Robert (1795–1832)

Poetic Background

"Spring has come, the birds are mating, and I am in love."

Please read about Robert in the notes to *Heimweh*. She came from an area called *Schwaben* (Swabia), and she wrote this poem in the dialect of that area, *schwäbisch* (Swabian). Swabia is far away to the south and west from Berlin, and its dialect sounds rather sweet and countrified to a Prussian citizen like Felix. Remember that until 1870 there was no unified nation of Germany.

A word is in order about German dialects. When Martin Luther translated the Bible from Latin into German in the 1520s, he created a standard form of written German that is now known as *Hochdeutsch* (High German). In daily life many Germans use regional languages that differ from the standard in various points of pronunciation, vocabulary and grammar. The differences are great enough that a visitor from the Rhineland, for instance, may not be able to understand a conversation between two Swabians, and vice versa. Even the influence of modern broadcast media has not eliminated regional dialects. They are sources of local pride and remain in vigorous use.

This poem is easily understood by non-Swabian Germans because it uses only some of the most noticeable traits of Swabian, such as the diminutive *-le* instead of *-lein*.

Line 1: *isch = ist* (is).

Line 2: *Wegle sin trucken = Weglein sind trocken* (little roads are dry).

Line 4: *zwitschern und locka* (twitter and entice): Robert is inconsistent in spelling verb forms, here and in Line 5. More typical of Swabian would be *zwitschre, locke, schlage*.

Line 5: *Bähm' = Bäume* (trees).

Line 6: *un i = und ich* (and I); *Veigele = Veilchen* (violet).

Interpretation

Out of a brief poem, Felix made a rather long song, using word repetition and ingenious musical variations.

The whole song is straightforward and cheerful. The *pp* at measure 63 brings an unexpected note of tenderness to the ending. The Italian-style cadenza must sound exuberant and as natural as a bird's song.

An example of Felix's skill in variation can be found in a tiny phrase of countermelody that occurs in each stanza. It is played by the right hand in measure 15, then by the left hand in measure 35, so that the right hand is free to carry on its bird-like chirping. The voice sings the same notes in measure 55, after the piano has taken over the main melody in measure 54. Other musical elements can likewise be traced through the song.

Some German recording artists alter the dialect words to High German, which is easily done.

Felix dated this song April 2, 1824; when he was 15. In the first edition there is a footnote: "The accompaniment of this song is actually written for a flute, a clarinet, two horns and a cello."

Frühlingslied

Friederike Robert

Felix Mendelssohn
Opus 8, No. 6

Literal Translation:

1) Now comes Spring; the sky is blue, the roads are dry, the breezes are mild.

lau. Jetzt kommt der Früh - ling, der Him-mel isch blau,_____

jetzt kommt der Früh-ling, der Him-mel isch blau, die Weg-le sin tru-cken, die Lüf-te geh'n

lau, jetzt_____ kommt_der_ Früh - ling!

(2.) Jetzt kommt der Früh-ling, die Vög-le im Wald_____

2) Now comes Spring; the little birds in the woods are twittering and enticing their mates.

(3.) Jetzt____ kommt der Früh-ling, die Bähm' schla-ge aus,

un i bring mei Schätz-le ein Vei-ge-le-strauss.

Jetzt kommt der

Früh - ling, die Bähm'___ schla-ge aus, jetzt kommt der Früh-ling, die Bähm' schla-ge

3) Now comes Spring; the trees are budding, and I'm bringing my darling a bunch of violets.

aus, un i bring mei Schätz-le ein Vei - ge - le - strauss, ein Vei - - - ge - le -

strauss, ein Vei - - - - ge - le -

strauss!

MAIENLIED

[mɑeənliːt]

(May Song)

man zɔl høːren zyːsəs zɪŋən
1 Man soll hören süßes Singen
One should hear sweet singing

ɪn den ɑoən yːbəral
2 In den Auen überall,
in the meadows everywhere,

liːblɪç hɛl gəzɑŋ ɛrklɪŋən
3 Lieblich hell Gesang erklingen,
lovely bright song ring-out,

forɑos voːr der nɑxtɪgal
4 Voraus vor der Nachtigall!
Ahead before the nightingale.

ʃɑoət ɑof den ɑŋər braet
5 Schauet auf den Anger breit,
Gaze on the meadow broad,

ʃɑoət an di lɪçtə hɑedə
6 Schauet an die lichte Haide,
gaze on the bright heath,

viː ziː ʃoːn zɪç mɪt dem klɑedə
7 Wie sie schon sich mit dem Kleide
how it already itself with the dress

tsu: dem mɑeən hat bəklɑet
8 Zu dem Maien hat bekleid't.
for the May has clothed.

mɑnçərhɑndə blyːməlɑen
9 Mancherhande Blümelein
Many-kinds-of little-flowers

lɑxən ɑos des mɑeən tɑo
10 Lachen aus des Maien Tau
laugh from the May's dew

ɪn der lɪçtən zɔnnə ʃaen
11 In der lichten Sonne Schein;
in the bright sun's radiance;

ʃøːnə tsaet tsuː veːrtər ʃɑo
12 Schöne Zeit zu werter Schau!
beautiful time for worthy display!

vas zɔl trøːstən miːr den muːt
13 Was soll trösten mir den Mut?
What should comfort for-me the courage?

da: mɪç tsvɪŋət hɛrtsənsʃveːrə
14 Da mich zwinget Herzensschwere,
Because me oppresses heart-heaviness:

bae deːr ɪç fiːl gɛrnə veːrə
15 Bei der ich viel gerne wäre,
with whom I much gladly would-be

das diː fɛrnə leːbən tuːt
16 Da die ferne leben tut.
that she distant live does.

Jacob von Warte (13th Century)
[jɑːkɔp fɔn vɑrtə]

Poetic Background

"All around me the world is ready for a spring festival, but my beloved is far away, so I am sad."

Von Warte was a nobleman from the area of Zurich, Switzerland. Four of his poems are preserved in a great collection of poetry that was written down in Zurich around 1304. The book is famous for its fanciful, brightly colored portraits of nobly born poets. It is sometimes called the Manesse Manuscript, after an early owner, and sometimes the Great Heidelberg Lieder-Manuscript, because it is now owned by the University of Heidelberg, Germany.

Von Warte was a *Minnesinger* or poet of courtly love. Minnesingers wrote idealistically about the power of love and about women they admired from afar. The women were never named because they were married and for that reason out of reach. All the poems were meant to be sung, but no authentic melody survives for this poem.

The text is a translation from the language of the Minnesingers, now called Middle High German. It uses some different letter forms and much less capitalization than modern German. As an example of Middle High German, here are lines 7 and 8 of the above poem in the original:

wie schone si sich mit ir kleide
gen dem meien hat bekleit.

The original poem has 15 eight-line stanzas, of which Felix used only the first two. The first edition uses the obsolete spelling *Mayenlied* for the title and incorrectly names the poet as Jacob von *der* Warte.

Interpretation

While it has a slightly quicker tempo, this song strongly resembles *Minnelied.* It is again in Felix's warm and gentle Classical mood, and again the first two measures of the vocal part form a unit that is heard twice more (measures 8–9 and measures 18–19), each time newly harmonized.

Felix put only three eighth-notes into measures 3 and 25. It was unusual for any composer of this period to take such a liberty with meter.

Maienlied

Jacob von Warte

Felix Mendelssohn
Opus 8, No. 7

Literal Translation:

1) One can hear sweet singing everywhere in the meadows, beautiful bright singing, led by the nightingale.
   Look out over the broad field, over the bright heath, and see how they are wearing their May dress.

2) Many kinds of little flowers are laughing in the Maytime dew under the bright sun— a fine time for such a show!
   What will comfort me? For a heavy heart oppresses me: the one whom I want to be with, lives far away from here.

Schau - et auf den An - ger breit, schau - et an die lich - te Hai - de,
Was soll trö - sten mir den Mut? da mich zwin - get Her - zens- schwe - re,

wie sie schon sich mit dem Klei - de zu __ dem Mai _ _ _ _ _
bei der ich viel ger - ne wä - re, dass __ die fer _ _ _ _

\- en hat __ be - kleid't.
\- ne le - ben _ tut.

 In November 1821, Felix was taken to Weimar to meet Goethe. The 73-year-old poet and the 12-year-old pianist became the best of friends. In this drawing, various members of the household have gathered in the evening to hear Felix play. Goethe, holding a book behind his back, looks over Felix's shoulder. Felix's teacher, Karl Friedrich Zelter, with his back to the artist, keeps a close watch over his student's playing.

This is an excerpt from a letter that Felix wrote to his family in Berlin:

"I play much more here than at home, seldom less than four hours, and sometimes six and even eight. Every afternoon Goethe opens his piano (a Streicher) with the words: 'I have not yet heard you today—now make a little noise for me.' And then he generally sits down beside me, and when I have finished (I usually extemporize), I ask for a kiss or I take one. You have no idea how good and kind he is to me, any more than you can imagine all the treasures in minerals, busts, prints, small statues and large original drawings, etc., which the polar star of poets possesses. His figure does not strike me as imposing; actually he is not much taller than father; but his bearing, his speech, and his name—these are imposing. The sound of his voice is tremendous, and he can shout like 10,000 warriors. His hair is not yet white, his step is firm, his way of speaking is mild."

Mendelssohn to his family, Weimar, 10 November 1821, *Letters*, ed. G. Seldon-Goth (New York: Pantheon Books, 1945).

HEXENLIED

[hɛksənli:t]

(Witch's Song)

di ʃvɑlbə fli:kt
1 **Die Schwalbe fliegt,**
The swallow flies,

der fry:lɪŋ zi:kt
2 **Der Frühling siegt,**
the spring is-victorious

ʊnt ʃpɛndət ʊns blu:mən tsʊm krɑntsə
3 **Und spendet uns Blumen zum Kranze!**
and donates to-us flowers for-the wreath.

balt huʃən vi:r
4 **Bald huschen wir**
Soon scuttle we

laez aos der ty:r
5 **Leis' aus der Tür,**
softly out the door

ʊnt fli:gən tsʊm prɛçtɪgən tɑntsə
6 **Und fliegen zum prächtigen Tanze!**
and fly to-the glorious dance!

aen ʃvɑrtsər bɔk
7 **Ein schwarzer Bock,**
A black billy-goat,

aen be:zənʃtɔk
8 **Ein Besenstock,**
a broomstick,

di o:fəngɑbəl der vɔkən
9 **Die Ofengabel, der Wocken,**
the oven-fork, the distaff,

raest ʊns gəʃvɪnt
10 **Reißt uns geschwind,**
tear us swiftly

vi: blɪts ʊnt vɪnt
11 **Wie Blitz und Wind,**
as lightning and wind

dʊrç zɑozəndə lʏftə tsʊm brɔkən
12 **Durch sausende Lüfte zum Brocken!**
through roaring winds to-the Brocken.

ʊm be:ltsəbu:p
13 **Um Beelzebub**
Around Beelzebub

tɑntst ʊnzər trʊp
14 **Tanzt unser Trupp**
dances our troop

ʊnt kʏst i:m di krɑllɪgən hɛndə
15 **Und küßt ihm die krallingen Hände!**
and kisses of-him the clawed hands.

aen gaesterʃvarm
16 **Ein Geisterschwarm**
a ghosts-swarm

fast ʊns baem arm
17 **Faßt uns beim Arm,**
grabs us by-the arm

ʊnt ʃvɪŋət ɪm tɑntsən di brɛndə
18 **Und schwinget im Tanzen die Brände!**
and swings in dancing the torches.

ʊnt be:ltsəbu:p
19 **Und Beelzebub**
And Beelzebub

fɛrhaest dem trʊp
20 **Verheißt dem Trupp**
promises to-the troop

der tɑntsəndən gɑ:bən aof gɑ:bən
21 **Der Tanzenden Gaben auf Gaben:**
of dancers gifts upon gifts;

zi: zɔllən ʃø:n
22 **Sie sollen schön**
they should beautiful

ɪn zaedə ge:n
23 **In Seide geh'n**
in silk walk

ʊnt tœpfə fɔl gɔldəs zɪç grɑ:bən
24 **Und Töpfe voll Goldes sich graben!**
and pots full gold for-themselves dig-up.

aen fɔøərdrax
25 **Ein Feuerdrach'**
A fiery-dragon

ʊmfli:gət das dax
26 **Umflieget das Dach**
around-flies the roof

ʊnt brɪŋət ʊns bʊtər ʊnt aeər
27 **Und bringet uns Butter und Eier!**
and brings us butter and eggs.

di naxba:rn dan ze:n
28 **Die Nachbarn dann sehn**
The neighbors then see

di fʊŋkən ve:n
29 **Die Funken wehn,**
the sparks blow

ʊnt ʃlɑ:gən aen krɔøts fo:r dem fɔøər
30 **Und schlagen ein Kreuz vor dem Feuer!**
and strike a cross before the fire.

31 **Die Schwalbe fliegt,**

32 **Der Frühling siegt,**

di blu:mən ɛrbly:ən tsʊm krɑntsə
33 **Die Blumen erblühen zum Kranze!**
The flowers bloom for-the wreath!

34	Bald huschen wir	juxhɑesə	tsʊm	prɛçtɪgən	tɑntsə
35	Leis' aus der Tür,	**36 Juchheissa! zum prächtigen Tanze!**			
		Hooray!	to-the	glorious	dance!

Ludewig Hölty (1748–1776)

Poetic Background

"We witches have a grand time on a spring night!"

Please read about Hölty in the notes to *Minnelied*.

Educated persons in Hölty's time no longer believed in witches, but in this poem Hölty was playing with the folk traditions about witchcraft, such as flying through the air on a broomstick. Only a century before, accusations of witchcraft were taken seriously; it was the era of the notorious Salem witch trials in Massachusetts.

Line 7: *Ein schwarzer Bock* (a black billy goat), *etc.*: these are things that witches use in working the magic that lets them fly through the air.

Line 12: *Brocken,* a peak in the Harz Mountains of central Germany and fabled gathering place of witches.

Line 19: *Beelzebub,* the name of a Philistine god (2 Kings 1:2), was later called "the prince of devils" (Matthew 12:24).

Line 30: *schlagen ein Kreuz* (strike a cross): having been awakened by all

the witches, the frightened neighbors protect themselves by waving a cross between themselves and the fiery dragon.

The original poem has six six-line stanzas. The sixth is identical to the first except that lines 33 and 36 read: *Die Blumen entblühn um die Wette!* (The flowers open up in a hurry!); and *Und lassen die Männer im Bette* (And leave our husbands in bed!) . Felix substituted the words given above and grouped the six poetic stanzas into three musical ones.

The poem appeared in *Gedichte* (Poems), edited by J. H. Voß and Count Friedrich Leopold Stolberg. (Hamburg: Bohn, 1783, copy at University of California at Los Angeles). The title page gives the poet's full name: Ludewig Heinrich Christoph Hölty.

Interpretation

This macabre and comical song is one of Felix's best, showing the lightness and sheer velocity that were so

distinctive in the Overture to *A Midsummer Night's Dream.*

Felix was a brilliant pianist and liked fast tempos; he surely had great fun playing this accompaniment. He also knew how to give the singer a good time: He always gave important words enough time and put them into the middle range. The long high notes are on repeated words and open vowels.

The moment of greatest mystery is at measure 46, where the accompaniment pauses on the tonic chord, in major mode and pianissimo. To keep the dynamic quiet, the pianist should hold down the bass note, playing other notes of the chord *tremolando* (repeating the higher and lower notes in each hand alternately at the speed of 16th notes) through measure 51. If the bass note is also repeated, the sound will probably be too loud on a modern piano.

In the first publication of Opus 8 this song was entitled *And'res Maienlied* (Another May Song) in contrast with the preceding song, *Maienlied.*

Hexenlied

Ludewig Hölty

Felix Mendelssohn
Opus 8, no. 8

8

(1.) Die Schwal - be fliegt, der Früh - ling siegt, und spen - det uns Blu-men zum Kran - ze!
(2. Um) Beel - ze-bub tanzt un - ser Trupp und küsst ihm die kral- li - gen Hän - de!

13

Bald hu-schen wir leis' aus der Tür, und flie - gen zum präch-ti - gen Tan - ze!
Ein Gei-ster-schwarm fasst uns beim Arm, und schwin - get im Tan-zen die Brän - de!

17

Ein schwar-zer Bock, ein Be - sen-stock, die O - fen-ga-bel, der Wo - cken,
Und Beel - ze - bub ver - heisst dem Trupp der Tan-zen-den Ga-ben auf Ga - ben:

Literal Translation:

1) The swallow flies, spring conquers and gives us flowers for our wreaths.
Soon we will scuttle softly out the door and fly to the glorious dance. A black billygoat, a broomstick, the oven-fork,
the distaff, tear us along swiftly as lightning, through roaring winds to our meeting place, Brocken Mountain.

2) We all dance around Beelzebub and kiss his clawed hands.
Ghosts in a swarm grab us by the arm and dance, swinging torches.
And Beelzebub promises everyone gifts and more gifts: they will all wear silks and dig up pots of gold.

3) A fiery dragon flies around the roof and brings us butter and eggs. The neighbors see the sparks and make the sign
of the cross to keep away the fire. The swallow flies, spring conquers and gives us flowers for our wreaths.
Soon we will scuttle softly out the door; hurray for the glorious dance!

ABENDLIED
[ɑːbəntliːt]

(Evening Song)

das tɑːgəverk ɪst |ʊpgətɑːn
1 **Das Tagewerk ist abgetan.**
The day-work is finished;

giːp vɑːtər dɑenən zeːgən
2 **Gib, Vater, deinen Segen!**
give, Father, thy blessing.

nuːn dʏrfən wiːr der ruːə nɑːn
3 **Nun dürfen wir der Ruhe nahn;**
Now may we to-the rest approach;

wiːr tɑːtən nɑx fermøːgən
4 **Wir taten nach Vermögen.**
we did according-to ability.

di hɔldə nɑxt ʊmhʏlt di velt
5 **Die holde Nacht umhüllt die Welt,**
The lovely night surrounds the world,

ʊnt ʃtɪllə herʃt ɪn dɔrf ʊnt felt
6 **Und Stille herrscht in Dorf und Feld.**
and quiet reigns in village and field.

ven duː gətrɔø fɔllɛndət hɑst
7 **Wenn du getreu vollendet hast,**
When you faithfully finished have

votsuː dɪç gɔt bəʃtɛltə
8 **Wozu dich Gott bestellte,**
whereto you God commanded

bəhɑːklɪç fyːlst duː dɑn di rɑst
9 **Behaglich fühlst du dann die Rast**
comfortable feel you then the rest

fɔm tuːn ɪn hɪts ʊnt kɛltə
10 **Vom Tun in Hitz' und Kälte.**
from doing in heat and cold.

ɑm hɪmməl glɛntst der |ɑːbəntʃtern
11 **Am Himmel glänzt der Abendstern**
In-the sky shines the evening-star

ʊnt tsɑekt nɔx bɛsrə rɑst fɔn fern
12 **Und zeigt noch bessre Rast von fern.**
and shows even better rest from far-away.

Johann Heinrich Voß (1751–1826)
[johɑn hɑenrɪç fɔs]

Poetic Background
"It is time for well-earned rest, which is a foretaste of Heaven."

The poet Voß studied at the University of Göttingen, where he belonged to the literary circle known as the *Hain* (grove). He wrote on many themes, some humorous or satirical, and experimented with complex poetic rhythms. Sometimes he even wrote musical notes over the first line of a poem to indicate the rhythm he had in mind. Please read more about him in the notes to *Minnelied*.

Line 11: *glänzt* (shines) is Felix's word; Voß wrote *blinkt* (gleams).

The original poem has seven six-line stanzas; Felix used only the first and fourth. Source: *Sämtliche Gedichte* (Collected Poems, [Königsberg: Universitats-Buchhandlung, 1825]), vol. 3.

Interpretation
Felix's choice of this quiet devotional poem expresses his love of stability and domesticity. Critics speak of the *Biedermeier* style, which in Germany meant idealizing the middle-class lifestyle, with its affirmation of material comfort and traditional values.

A love of home was certainly one side of Felix's personality, and he probably thought of this calm and quiet song being sung at home in a family circle. Public song recitals were not yet part of conventional concert life.

The beauties of this song are subtle ones: the phrase ending on a minor ninth (measure 8, beat 3); the dark chromaticism that conveys the feeling of night (measures 11–12). In spite of a mood of reverent calm, Felix avoids monotony by varying the accompaniment and avoiding the tonic harmony for several measures at a time.

In the first edition the first stanza is printed with the music and the second stanza is printed separately as a poem.

Literal Translation:

1) The day's work is done. Father, give your blessing! Now we may go to rest; we have done the best we could. The lovely night enfolds the world and quiet reigns in town and field.

2) When you have faithfully completed what God has given you to do, then your rest feels comfortable after work in heat and cold. The evening star shines in the heavens and shows us an even better rest that is to come.

Abendlied

Original key: E♭ major

Johann Heinrich Voß

Felix Mendelssohn
Opus 8, No. 9

(1.) Das Ta - ge - werk ist ab - ge - tan. Gib
(2.) Wenn du ge - treu voll - en - det hast, wo -

Va - ter dei - nen Se - gen! Nun dür - fen wir der Ru - he nah'n; wir
zu dich Gott be - stell - te, be - hag - lich fühlst du dann die Rast vom

ta - ten nach Ver - mö - gen. Die hol - de Nacht um - hüllt die Welt, und
Tun in Hitz' und Käl - te. Am Him - mel glänzt der A - bend - stern und

Stil - le herrscht in Dorf und Feld.
zeigt noch bess - re Rast von fern.

ROMANZE

[romɑntsə]

(Romance)

ɑenmɑ:l ɑos zɑenən blɪkən
1 Einmal aus seinen Blicken,
Once from his glances,

fɔn zɑenəm zy:sən mʊnt
2 Von seinem süßen Mund,
from his sweet mouth,

zɔl gru:s ʊnt kʊs ɛrkvɪkən
3 Soll Gruß und Kuß erquicken
may greeting and kiss comfort

dɛs hɛrtsəns try:bən grʊnt
4 Des Herzens trüben Grund.
the heart's somber depth.

ɪç kɑn i:n nɪçt fɛrgɛsən
5 Ich kann ihn nicht vergessen,
I can him not forget,

ɪç kɑn ɛs nɪçt bərɔøn
6 Ich kann es nicht bereu'n,
I can it not regret.

ɪç zʏndgə nɪçt fɛrmɛsən
7 Ich sünd'ge nicht vermessen,
I sin not audaciously;

der hɪmməl vɪrt fɛrtsɑen
8 Der Himmel wird verzeih'n!
the heaven will forgive.

Anonymous

Poetic Background

"He is on my mind all the time, but that's not a great sin!"

The first edition of Opus 8 said that this poem was translated from Spanish, which may not be true. Years later, Felix's friend, Eduard Devrient, wrote that this song was originally part of Felix's opera *Die Hochzeit des Camacho* (Camacho's Wedding), Op. 10, although the song was not kept in the finished score. Since it is believed that Carl Klingemann wrote the libretto of the opera (based on a subject from the works of Cervantes), he may also have written this poem.

The title *Romanze* simply means a lyrical, usually sentimental song.

Interpretation

This song presents the vivid personality of a passionate young Spanish woman. Her unrequited love calls for a minor key and a moderately slow tempo, but her irrepressible spirit emerges in floods of coloratura singing. The style is comparable to Spanish music of the early 1800s.

The singer has a choice of which high notes to sing. The first two beats of measure 19 and the first beat of measure 22 must be stretched enough to allow time to take breaths. In each case, the tempo resumes on the next beat.

Romanze

Anonymous

Felix Mendelssohn
Opus 8, No. 10

Ein - mal aus sei - nen Bli - cken, von _ sei - nem sü - ssen _

Mund, soll Gruss und Kuss er - qui - cken _ des _ Her - zens trü - ben

Grund. Ich kann _ ihn _ nicht ver - ges - sen, ich kann _ es _ nicht be -

Literal Translation:

Just once from his eyes and from his sweet mouth I want to receive a greeting and a kiss that would comfort
the somber depths of my heart. I cannot forget him; I am not sorry. My sin is not too great; Heaven will forgive me.

IM GRÜNEN
[ɪm gry̠ːnən]

(In the Open)

1 **Willkommen im Grünen!**
vɪlkɔmmən ɪm gry̠ːnən
Welcome in-the green!

2 **Der Himmel ist blau,**
der hɪmməl ɪst blɑo
The sky is blue

3 **Und blumig die Au!**
ʊnt blu̠ːmɪç di ɑo
and flowery the meadow.

4 **Der Lenz ist erschienen!**
der lɛnts ɪst |ɛrʃi̠ːnən
The spring has appeared.

5 **Er spiegelt sich hell**
eːr ʃpiːgəlt zɪç hɛl
It mirrors itself brightly

6 **Am luftigen Quell**
am lu̠ftɪgən kvɛl
in-the airy spring.

7 **Im Grünen!**

8 **Willkommen im Grünen!**

9 **Das Vögelchen springt**
dɑs føːgəlçən ʃprɪŋt
The little-bird leaps

10 **Auf Sprossen und singt:**
ɑof ʃprɔsən ʊnt zɪŋt
on branches and sings,

11 **Der Lenz ist erschienen!**
der lɛnts ɪst |ɛrʃi̠ːnən
the spring has appeared.

12 **Ihm säuselt der West**
iːm zɔøzəlt der vɛst
To-it whispers the west-wind

13 **Ums heimliche Nest**
ʊms hɑemlɪçə nɛst
around-the hidden nest...

14 **Im Grünen!**

Johann Heinrich Voß (1751–1826)

Poetic Background
"How good it is to be outdoors after being closed in all winter!"

Please read about the poet in the notes to *Abendlied*.

Line 4: *Lenz* (spring) is a poetic word; *Frühling* (spring) is more usual.

Line 4: *erschienen* rhymes with *Grünen*. Notice that in German verse the rhyme between [yː] and [iː] is accepted, but [yː] and [uː] do not rhyme.

Line 6: *luftigen Quell* (airy spring): "airy" is an odd word to describe a spring of water, but it carries the sense of being outdoors in the fresh air.

Line 10: *Auf Sprossen* (on branches) is the poet's own revision found in the 1825 edition; the 1795 edition had *Durch Blätter* (through leaves).

The original poem contained eight seven-line stanzas. The first line of each is *Willkommen im Grünen,* the fourth line rhymes with it, and the seventh line is *Im Grünen.* Felix used only the first two stanzas. The poem is found in *Gedichte* (Poems, [Königsberg: Nicolovius, 1795]), vol. 2.

Interpretation
A traditional German instrument for outdoor music making is the *Wald-horn* (forest horn), which resembles a French horn, built smaller and without keys. Typically, several persons play together, costumed in forest green. The introduction to this song imitates the sound of a fanfare played by such a group. This kind of musical texture reminds German listeners of fresh air and the out-of-doors before even a word of the text has been heard.

If the vocal tessitura seems too high in the original key, it is partly because pianos are tuned higher now than in Felix's time. If the song is performed in E-flat, the result will be close to Felix's expectations.

Im Grünen

Johann Heinrich Voß

Felix Mendelssohn
Opus 8, No. 11

Literal Translation:

1) Welcome to the outdoors! The sky is blue and the meadow is in bloom.
   Spring has come, reflected in the bubbling wellspring out in the open.

2) Welcome to the outdoors! The little bird leaps from branch to branch and sings, "Spring has come."
   The gentle west wind whispers around its hidden nest, out in the open.

SULEIKA UND HATEM

[zulɑeka ʊnt hɑːtɛm]

(Suleika and Hatem)

SULEIKA:

ɑn dɛs lʊstgən brʊnnəns rɑnt
1 **An des lust'gen Brunnens Rand,**
on   the   cheerful   fountain's   rim,

der   ɪn vɑsərfɛːdən   ʃpiːlt
2 **Der   in Wasserfäden   spielt,**
which   in   water-threads   plays,

vʊst ɪç nɪçt vas fɛst mɪç hiːlt
3 **Wußt ich nicht, was   fest   mich hielt;**
knew I   not   what firmly me   held,

dɔx dɑː vɑːr fɔn dɑenər hɑnt
4 **Doch da   war   von   deiner Hand**
but   there was   from your   hand

mɑenə ʃɪfər   laez   gətsoːgən
5 **Meine Chiffer   leis'   gezogen,**
my   code-word quietly drawn.

niːdər blɪkt ɪç diːr gəvoːgən
6 **Nieder blickt' ich,   dir   gewogen.**
Down   looked I,   to-you well-disposed.

hiːr ɑm ɛndə dɛs kɑnɑːls
7 **Hier,   am   Ende des   Canals**
Here at-the end   of-the canal

der   gərɑetən   hɑoptǀalle:
8 **Der   gereihten   Hauptallee,**
of-the   straight-lined   main-avenue,

blɪk ɪç viːdər ɪn di høː
9 **Blick' ich wieder in   die Höh',**
look   I   again   into the height

ʊnt dɑː ze: ɪç ɑːbermɑls
10 **Und da   seh' ich abermals**
and   there see I   another-time

mɑenə lɛtərn fɑen gətsoːgən
11 **Meine Lettern fein   gezogen:**
my   letters   finely drawn,

blɑebə blɑebə miːr gəvoːgən
12 **Bleibe! bleibe mir   gewogen!**
"Stay,   stay   to-me   well-disposed."

HATEM:

møːgə vɑsər ʃprɪŋənt vɑllənt
13 **Möge Wasser springend, wallend,**
May   water,   leaping,   bubbling,

di tsyprɛsən diːr gəʃteːn
14 **Die Zypressen dir   gestehn:**
the   cypress   to-you confess:

fɔn zulɑeka tsuː zulɑeka
15 **Von   Suleika zu   Suleika**
from   Suleika to   Suleika

ɪst mɑen kɔmmən ʊnt mɑen geːn
16 **Ist mein Kommen und mein Gehn.**
is   my   coming   and my   going.

Johann Wolfgang von Goethe (1749–1832)
[johɑn vɔlfgaŋ fɔn gøːtə]

Poetic Background

The young woman says, "When I looked at the surface of the bubbling fountain, I saw my name in your handwriting; the same occurred when I looked at the dark cypress trees." The old man replies, "These things tell you that all my life revolves around you."

At 65 years of age, Goethe was recognized as the greatest poet of the German language. Nevertheless, a new way of writing opened up for him in 1814 when he read a German translation of poems by Hafiz, a Persian poet of the 1300s. Goethe responded by writing *West-östlicher Divan*. The Persian word *divan* means a collection of poems. Goethe could not write an authentically oriental divan, so he called his "western-oriental."

In *Divan* the old man Hatem represents Goethe himself. The young woman Suleika represents Marianne von Willemer, a gifted ballet dancer and poet. She was the object of Goethe's last passionate but unfulfilled love affair.

Line 8: *gereihten* here means lined with a row of trees, which is made clear when Hatem mentions cypresses (line 14). The scene, with fountain, canal, and tree-lined avenue, is exotic and luxurious.

Line 9: *Höh'* rhymes with *Haup-tallee* (line 8). Notice that in German verse [øː] may rhyme with [eː], not with [oː].

Interpretation

Please read in the preface about the visits Felix and Fanny made to Goethe. Probably these events gave Fanny the courage to publish this Goethe setting. Felix did not set any of Goethe's poetry to music until after Goethe and Zelter had died.

Fanny placed expressive markings in Italian over the voice parts; observe them carefully. *A piacere* (at pleasure) at measure 40, means to take extra time as desired.

Suleika und Hatem

J. W. von Goethe

Fanny Hensel
Opus 8, No. 12

Literal Translation:

1) Suleika says: "Seated on the edge of the cheerful fountain with its playing strands of water,
   I did not know what was fascinating me; yet there on the surface was my secret name, written as you write it.
   I gazed downward, loving you.

2) "Here at the end of the canal that borders the main avenue, I look up to the cypress trees and see again
   the characters of my name finely drawn, saying, 'Keep on loving me!'"

3) Hatem says: "May the leaping, bubbling water and the cypresses, too, bear my confession to you: from Suleika to Suleika is all my coming and going."

FRAGE

[frɑːgə]

(Question)

ɪst ɛs vɑːr
1 **Ist es wahr? Ist es wahr?**
Is it true

das duː ʃteːts dɔrt ɪn dem lɑopgaŋ
2 **Daß du stets dort in dem Laubgang,**
that you always there in the leafy-path,

an der vɑenvant mɑenər harst
3 **an der Weinwand meiner harrst?**
by the vine-wall for-me wait,

ʊnt den moːnt\ʃaen ʊnt diː ʃtɛrnlaen
4 **und den Mondschein und die Sternlein**
and the moonlight and the little-stars

ɑox nɑx miːr bəfrɑːkst
5 **auch nach mir befragst?**
also about me question?

ʃprɪç vas ɪç fyːlə
6 **Ist es wahr? Sprich! Was ich fühle,**
Speak! What I feel,

das bəgrɑeft nuːr diː ɛs mɪtfyːlt
7 **das begreift nur, die es mitfühlt,**
that understands only who it with-feels

ʊnt diː trɔø miːr eːvɪç blɑept
8 **und die treu mir ewig bleibt.**
and who true to-me eternally remains.

"H. Voss" (Felix Mendelssohn)

Poetic Background
"Do you love as much as I do?"

The first edition of Opus 9 identified the poet of this song and *Scheidend* as "H. Voss." In a music periodical, A. B. Marx, a close friend of Felix, revealed that Felix was the real poet. Sebastian Hensel, Fanny's son, later wrote that Felix had written both the words and music of *Frage* on June 6, 1827, while vacationing near Potsdam. (The poems were not written by J. H. Voß, whose poetry Felix set in Opus 8.)

Line 7: *die* is feminine; a woman who sings this song might change the word to *der* here and in line 8.

Because the poem is unrhymed and otherwise unpublished, one cannot be sure of its original form. The eight-line arrangement shown above is conjectural.

Interpretation
This song begins Opus 9 on a level of intense self-expression not found in Felix's songs in Opus 8. It seems almost as if the publication of Opus 8 allowed Felix to realize what Fanny's songs had that his lacked. Only a few months later he took a leap forward in self-expression.

It is very likely that Felix was in love at age 18, as this song implies, but we do not know with whom. He was attracted to many women and they to him, but he seldom mentioned romance in the letters that survive.

The questioning phrase that opens this song is so distinctive and dramatic that Felix used it several months later as the basis of a string quartet, also in A major.

The dynamic markings may be somewhat misleading. In measure 10 a pair of crescendo-diminuendo signs is centered over the second note alone, when obviously the dynamic rise and fall should extend over several beats. The same marking occurs in measure 20 in spite of the *cresc.* printed through two beats in the piano part; the marking merely indicates the peak of a larger rise and fall.

Frage

"Voss" (Felix Mendelssohn)

Felix Mendelssohn
Opus 9, No. 1

Literal Translation:

Is it true that you are always there in the leafy path by the grape arbor, waiting for me?
And that you ask the moon and the stars about me? Speak! What I feel can be understood only by someone who feels it, too,
and who will remain true to me forever.

GESTÄNDNIS
[gəʃtɛntnɪs]

(Confession)

kɛnst du: nɪçt das glu:tfɛrlɑŋən
1 **Kennst du nicht das Glutverlangen,**
Know you not the fever-longing,

di:zə kva:l ʊnt di:zə lʊst
2 **Diese Qual und diese Lust,**
this agony and this delight,

di: mɪt hɔfən ʊnt mɪt bɑŋən
3 **Die mit Hoffen und mit Bangen**
which with hoping and with fearing

vo:gət dʊrç di ɛ̞ŋə brʊst
4 **Woget durch die enge Brust?**
surges through the cramped breast?

zi:st du: dɛn nɪçt vi: ɪç be:bə
5 **Siehst du denn nicht, wie ich bebe,**
See you then not how I tremble,

ʃaen ɪç lɛçəlnt ɑox ʊnt kalt
6 **Schein ich lächelnd auch und kalt,**
seem I smiling also and cold?

vi: ɪç rɪŋə vi: ɪç ʃtre:bə
7 **Wie ich ringe, wie ich strebe**
How I wrestle, how I strive

ge:gən daenə ɑlgəvalt
8 **Gegen deine Allgewalt?**
against your omnipotence?

a:nst du: nɪçts fɔn maenən ʃmɛrtsən
9 **Ahnst du nichts von meinen Schmerzen,**
Sense you nothing of my pains?

hast du: mɪtlaet nɪçt fy:r mɪç
10 **Hast du Mitleid nicht fur mich,**
Have you sympathy not for me?

ʃprɪçt ɪm ʊnʔɛntvaetən hɛrtsən
11 **Spricht im unentweihten Herzen**
Speaks in-the undisturbed heart

kaenə ʃtɪmə dɛn fy:r mɪç
12 **Keine Stimme denn für mich?**
no voice then for me?

las di kva:l mɪç nɪçt fɛrtse:rən
13 **Laß die Qual mich nicht verzehren,**
Let the agony me not devour;

ax maria zae dɔx maen
14 **Ach Maria, sei doch mein!**
ah Maria, be indeed mine!

di:r nu:r vɪl ɪç ʔangəhø:rən
15 **Dir nur will ich angehören,**
To-you only want I to-belong,

ɪc vɪl gants daen ʔaegən zaen
16 **Ich will ganz dein eigen sein!**
I want entirely your own to-be!

Eduard Devrient (1801–1877)
[e:duart defri:nt]

Poetic Background

"Can you see how I am suffering for love of you?"

The first edition of this song did not name the poet, probably by his own wish. He was Eduard Devrient, a well known singer and actor and a frequent visitor at the Mendelssohn home. It was Devrient who urged Felix to undertake the bold project of reviving J. S. Bach's *St. Matthew Passion* in 1829, when no one had performed it for a hundred years. Devrient worked closely with Felix on the difficult diplomatic and practical preparations for the concert, and he himself sang the role of Jesus.

Devrient also wrote two opera li-

brettos for Felix, but neither was used.

Line 6: *Schein ich ... = obwohl ich... scheine* (even if I seem...).

Line 8: *Allgewalt* (omnipotence), is a divine attribute; the poet loves to the point of idolatry.

Line 11: *unentweihten* (undisturbed or even unprofaned); the serenity and purity of her heart have not yet been disturbed by his love.

Interpretation

This song is linked to the preceding song by key, meter, and mood, as well as by the identity of the first few notes of the voice part. The song is not dated, but it must have been written soon after *Frage*, when Felix had not

yet exhausted his fascination with the three-note-question motif he had discovered.

"With expressive fire, but in a moderate tempo," is the unusual combination of instructions for this song, which continues the passionate personal expression that began in *Frage*.

No doubt the song was written with Devrient's baritone voice in mind. He must have enjoyed making contrasts between soft and loud, for peaks of loudness occur five times in each stanza. The softer phrases are by no means calm; one feels in them that the poet makes an effort to control himself, so as not to overwhelm the beloved with his declaration.

Geständnis

Eduard Devrient

Felix Mendelssohn
Opus 9, No. 2

Literal Translation:

1) Do you not know the burning desire, the agony and delight that surge, with hope and fear, through my aching bosom?

   Do you not see how I am trembling, even if I seem smiling and calm?

   Do you not see how I struggle against your all-encompassing power?

2) Do you not sense my pain, do you have no sympathy for me? Is there no voice within your serene heart that speaks for me?

   Do not let this agony devour me! Ah, Maria, be mine! I want to belong only to you and to be entirely your own!

WARTEND
[vɑrtənt]

(Waiting)

1 **Sie trug einen Falken auf ihrer Hand,**
zi: tru:k ɑenən fɑlkən ɑof i:rər hɑnt
She carried a falcon on her hand

2 **Und hat ihn über den See gesandt.**
ʊnt hɑt i:n y:ber den ze: gəzɑnt
and has him over the lake sent.

3 **Komme du bald!**
kɔmmə du: bɑlt
Come you soon!

4 **Er kam mit dem Falken wohl über den See**
e:r kɑ:m mɪt dem fɑlkən vo:l y:bər den ze:
He came with the falcon indeed over the lake

5 **Und blies ins Hüfthorn vor Lust und Weh.**
ʊnt bli:s ɪns hyfthɔrn fo:r lʊst ʊnt ve:
and blew into-the hip-horn for joy and sorrow.

6 **Komme du bald!**

7 **Der Falk flog weit in Wald und Nacht,**
der fɑlk flo:k vɑet ɪn vɑlt ʊnt nɑxt
The falcon flew far in forest and night;

8 **Vom Morgentraum ist das Fräulein erwacht.**
fɔm mɔrgəntrɑom ɪst das frɔølɑen ɛrvɑxt
From-the morning-dream is the young-woman awakened.

9 **Komme du bald!**

Johann Gustav Droysen (1808–1884)
[johɑn gʊstaf drɔøzən]

Poetic Background

"She sent a falcon across the lake to look for her lover. He came back across the lake with the falcon to look for her. The falcon came to waken her." The story ends there.

Droysen was a friend of the Mendelssohns who, like so many others, was attracted by their generous hospitality and intellectual brilliance. He studied at the University of Berlin, where he was later a professor of classical philology. He also wrote major works on German history.

Line 1: *einen Falken* (a falcon) is a trained hunting bird that perches on its master's leather glove. The sight of a woman with a falcon is unusual. She is probably a lady, a landowner, a self-sufficient sportswoman. She has power to command the falcon.

Line 3: *"Komme du bald"* is the message the lady sends with the falcon and the message the hunter blows with his horn (line 6). It is also the message the lady receives when the falcon awakens her (line 9).

Line 5: *Hüfthorn* means a hunting horn slung from his belt, on his hip. The piano plays open fifths (measure 9) and horn fifths (measures 11–12) which musically symbolize hunting and an outdoor life.

The subtitle *Romanze* may mean a lyrical song, just as in *Romanze, Op. 8, No. 10.* What the two songs have in common is that each purports to come from far away: the earlier song from Spain and this one from the Middle Ages.

Interpretation

Several musical characteristics show that Felix was thinking of times long past: minor key, angular melody, minimal accompaniment. *Erntelied* had these same characteristics, but *Wartend* makes much greater demands on the singer with its quick tempo, sustained high notes and hushed final stanza. The dynamics are clearly spelled out.

The end of the story is left untold; only a final major chord hints that the lovers are rejoined.

The manuscript of this song was dated April 3, 1829, according to Stoner.

Wartend
(Romanze)

Johann Gustav Droysen

Felix Mendelssohn
Opus 9, No. 3

(1.) Sie_ trug ei-nen Fal-ken auf ih-rer Hand, und
(2.) Er_ kam mit dem Fal-ken wohl ü-ber den See und

hat ihn_ ü-ber den See ge-sandt, ü-ber den See_____ ge-sandt.
blies ins_ Hüft-horn vor Lust und Weh, vor Lust_____ und Weh.

Kom-me du bald,_____ kom-me du bald!_
Kom-me du bald,_____ kom-me du bald!_

Literal Translation:

1) She carried a falcon on her hand and she sent it across the lake. Come back soon!

2) He came with the falcon across the lake and blew on his hunting horn for joy and sorrow. Come back soon!

16

(3.) Der __ Falk flog weit in __ Wald und Nacht, vom Mor- gen -traum ist das

pp   sempre *pp*   *mezza voce*   *ri -*

20

Fräu - lein er-wacht,   ist das Fräu - lein er- wacht.   Kom - me,

tar - - - *dan* - - - *do*   *f* tempo

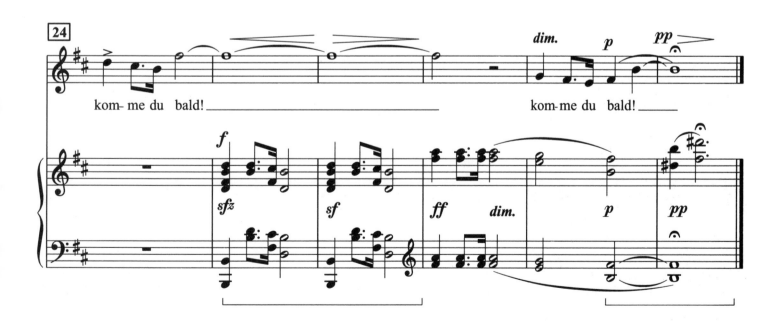

24

kom- me du bald! _____ kom- me du bald! _____

dim.   *p*   *pp*

3) The falcon flew far through the forest at night; the woman woke from her morning dream. Come back soon!

IM FRÜHLING
[ɪm fryːlɪŋ]

(In Spring)

iːr fryːlɪŋstrʊŋknən bluːmən
1 **Ihr frühlingstrunknen Blumen,**
You spring-drunk flowers,

iːr bɔømə moːntdʊrçblɪŋkət
2 **Ihr Bäume, monddurchblinket!**
you trees, moon-through-glanced,

iːr kœnts nɪçt zɑːgən ʊnt zaet ʃtʊm
3 **Ihr könnt's nicht sagen und seid stumm,**
you can nothing say and are silent.

viː syːs iːr ʃvɛlkt ʊnt trɪŋkət
4 **Wie süß ihr schwelgt und trinket!**
How sweetly you revel and drink!

ɪç trɪŋk ʊnt ʃvɛlgə mɪt ɔøç
5 **Ich trink' und schwelge mit euch**
I drink and revel with you

ʊnt zɪŋs ɪn hɛllər fryːlɪŋslʊst
6 **Und sing's in heller Frühlingslust.**
and sing-it in bright spring-delight.

oː viː miːr |aog ʊnt vɑŋə glyːt
7 **O wie mir Aug' und Wange glüht!**
O how to-me eye and cheek glow!

viː heːpt ʊnt zeːnt zɪç maenə brʊst
8 **Wie hebt und sehnt sich meine Brust!**
How rises and longs itself my breast!

duː zeːnzʊxtlɔøçtənt moːntlɪçt
9 **Du sehnsuchtleuchtend Mondlicht,**
you longing-shining moonlight,

iːr friːtlɪç hɛllən ʃtɛrnə
10 **Ihr friedlich hellen Sterne!**
You peaceful bright stars,

blɪkt tsuː den bluːmən ʃtɪl hɛrɑp
11 **Blickt zu den Blumen still herab,**
you-gaze to the flowers silently downward,

ɔøç blaept der fryːlɪŋ fɛrnə
12 **Euch bleibt der Frühling ferne!**
from-you remains the spring distant.

miːr blyːt ʊnt glyːt di roːzə
13 **Mir blüht und glüht die Rose**
For-me blooms and glows the rose

ʊnt miːr di frɪʃə fryːlɪŋsprɑxt
14 **Und mir die frische Frühlingspracht!**
and for-me the fresh spring-glory.

al maenə trɔømə zɪnt ɛrfylt
15 **All' meine Träume sind erfüllt,**
All my dreams are fulfilled;

nuːn ɪst dem hɛrtsən ruː gəbrɑxt
16 **Nun ist dem Herzen Ruh' gebracht.**
now is to-the heart rest brought.

Johann Gustav Droysen (1808–1884)

Poetic Background

"On this fragrant, moonlit night it seems that spring has come just for me."

In early editions of Opus 9 this poem was anonymous, but it is now known that the poet was Droysen. Please read about him in the notes to *Wartend.* In a letter first published in 1959, Felix wrote to Droysen asking for some changes in the poem. After apologizing for his request, Felix said, "By God, Voss does not know what else to do. Help!" Droysen must have known that "Voss" was Felix's pen name for the song *Frage.* Felix was saying that he himself did not know how to alter Droysen's poem and needed his help.

Interpretation

In spite of the nocturnal scene, the mood is impetuous and exalted. Although the poem is undistinguished, this is one of Felix's strongest, most vigorous songs.

The tempo is quick but easy to maintain, with only one or two syllables of text in each measure. At measures 47–48 the tempo slows considerably, allowing for an ample breath at the punctuation in measure 48. The tempo resumes in measure 49.

The grace note in measure 54 should probably be treated as an appoggiatura, that is, as a full eighth note. It is not clear why Felix used this old-fashioned notation.

In the first edition the second stanza ends with the syllable *-bracht* printed in measure 55 and a whole rest for the voice in measure 56. This seems illogical, and Rietz was probably correct to change it in the complete works to the form given here.

Im Frühling

Johann Gustav Droysen

Felix Mendelssohn
Opus 9, No. 4

Literal Translation:

1) You flowers that are drunk with spring, you trees that are pierced by moonlight, you are silent and dumb.
   How sweetly you revel and drink! I do so, too, and sing out with the bright joy of spring!
   O how my eyes and cheeks glow, how my breast rises with feelings of longing!

2) You moonlight that is aglow with longing, you stars that are peaceful and bright, you gaze down on the flowers;
   you remain distant from spring. The rose blooms and glows for me, spring's glory is all for me!
   All my dreams are fulfilled; now my heart is at peace.

IM HERBST

[ɪm hɛrpst]

(In Autumn)

ax vi: ʃnɛl di tɑːgə fliːən		
1 Ach wie schnell die Tage fliehen,		
Ah, how quickly the days flee,		

vo: di zeːnzuxt nɔø ˈɛrvɑxt
2 Wo die Sehnsucht neu erwacht,
when the longing new awakens,

vo: di bluːmən viːdər blyːən
3 Wo die Blumen wieder blühen
when the flowers again bloom

ʊnt der fryːlɪŋ viːdər lɑxt
4 Und der Frühling wieder lacht!
and the spring again laughs.

ɑllə vɔnnə zɔll ɛrʃteːən
5 Alle Wonne soll erstehen,
All delight should rise-from-the-dead,

ɪn ˈɛrfʏllʊŋ ˈɑlləs geːən
6 In Erfüllung Alles gehen.
into fulfillment everything go.

zeːt di tɑːgə geːn ʊnt kɔmmən
7 Seht die Tage geh'n und kommen,
See the days go and come,

tsiːn foːryːbər blyːtənʃveːr
8 Zieh'n vorüber blütenschwer,
pass by blossom-heavy;

zɔmmərlʊst ɪst bɑlt fɛrglɔmmən
9 Sommerlust ist bald verglommen,
summer-joy has soon died-away.

ʊnt der hɛrpstvɪnt raoʃt dɑːheːr
10 Und der Herbstwind rauscht daher.
and the autumn-wind rushes away.

ax das rɛçtə blyːn ʊnt gryːnən
11 Ach, das rechte Blühn und Grünen,
Ah, the real blooming and turning-green,

ɛs ɪst viːdər nɪçt ˈɛrʃiːnən
12 Es ist wieder nicht erschienen!
it has again not appeared.

Carl Klingemann (1798–1862)
[kɑrl klɪŋəmɑn]

Poetic Background

"How quickly the time has passed! It is already fall, and the hopes and longings I had in spring were never fulfilled."

Carl Klingemann, a native of Hanover and a fine amateur musician, was Felix's best friend when they were teenagers in Berlin. By the end of 1827 he was already living in London, where he embarked on a diplomatic career. When Felix visited Great Britain in 1829, Klingemann helped to introduce him to English society. The two friends toured Scotland together, where Felix was inspired to write his *Hebrides Overture*. Felix wrote more songs to Klingemann's texts than those of any other poet.

Interpretation

Im Herbst was composed in Berlin on March 23, 1827 (perhaps before any other song in Opus 9) after Opus 8 had been submitted to the publisher.

The song is constructed formally in the same way as the first song in Opus 8: the melody of measures 1–2 is repeated in measures 5–6 and again in measures 15–16, each time with a different conclusion. Within this familiar pattern are subtleties that are easily overlooked. The contrasting section that begins in measure 9 has the melody in the accompaniment. The chromatic note in measure 13 and the unsupported dissonance in measure 14 on the word *schnell* are unexpected flashes of color, as is the unprepared dissonance in measure 22. The quickly flowing melody of the piano postlude (measures 17 and 26) symbolizes the passing of spring.

Im Herbst

Carl Klingemann

Felix Mendelssohn
Opus 9, No. 5

(1.) Ach, wie schnell die Ta - ge flie - hen, wo die Sehn - sucht neu er - wacht,
(2.) Seht die Ta - ge geh'n und kom - men, zieh'n vor - ü - ber blü - ten - schwer,

wo die Blu - men wie - der blü - hen und der Früh - ling wie - der lacht!
Som - mer-lust ist bald ver - glom-men, und der Herbst - wind rauscht da - her.

Literal Translation:

1) Ah, how quickly pass the days when longing wakens anew, when flowers bloom again and spring laughs again,
   when joys are expected to rise from the dead and everything should reach fulfillment.

2) Watch the days come and go, passing by heavy with flowers; summer delights are soon faded and the autumn wind roars in.
   Ah, the true blooming and flourishing has again failed to come!

9

Al - le Won - ne soll er - ste - hen, in Er - füll - ung Al - les ge - hen.
Ach, das rech - te Blühn und Grü - nen, es ist wie - der nicht er - schie - nen!

13

Ach, wie schnell, ach, wie schnell, ach, wie schnell die Ta - ge flie - hen, wo die Sehn - sucht
wie - der nicht, wie - der nicht! Ach, wie schnell die Ta - ge flie - hen, wo die Sehn - sucht

18

1. neu er - wacht!
2. neu er - wacht! Ach, wie schnell,

23

ach, wie schnell, ach, wie schnell sie _ flie - hen!

SCHEIDEND
[ʃɑedənt]

(Parting)

vi: zo: gəlɪndə di flu:t bəve:kt
1 Wie so gelinde die Flut bewegt!
How very gently the stream moves,

vi: zi: zo: ru:ɪç den nɑxən trɛ:kt
2 Wie sie so ruhig den Nachen trägt!
how it so quietly the boat bears.

fɛrn li:kt das le:bən das ju:gəntlɑnt
3 Fern liegt das Leben, das Jugendland,
Distant lies the life, the youth-land,

fɛrn li:kt der ʃmɛrts der dɔrt mɪç bɑnt
4 Fern liegt der Schmerz, der dort mich band,
distant lies the pain which there me held.

zɑnft tra:kt mɪç flu:tən tsʊm fɛrnən lɑnt
5 Sanft tragt mich, Fluten, zum fernen Land!
Gently bear me, streams, to-the distant land!

dro:bən der ʃtɛrnə ʃtɪllər lɔrt
6 Droben der Sterne stiller Ort,
Overhead the stars' silent place,

ʊntən der ʃtro:m fli:st fɔrt ʊnt fɔrt
7 Unten der Strom fließt fort und fort.
below the river flows on and on.

vo:l va:rst du: raeç maen ju:gəntlɑnt
8 Wohl warst du reich, mein Jugendland,
Truly were you rich, my youth-land!

vo:l wa:r ɛs zy:s vas dɔrt mɪç bɑnt
9 Wohl war es süß, was dort mich band,
Truly was it sweet, what there me bound

zɑnft tra:kt mɪç flu:tən tsʊm fɛrnən lɑnt
10 Sanft tragt mich, Fluten, zum fernen Land!
Gently bear me, streams, to-the distant land!

"H. Voss" (Felix Mendelssohn)

Poetic Background
"Leaving the homeland of my childhood behind, I am thinking of both pain and joy that I knew there."

Please read about this pen name of Felix's in the notes to *Frage.*

Interpretation
For the first time, Felix uses a German expression for the tempo: *Sehr ruhig* (very calmly). Beethoven and Schubert pioneered the use of German expressions for tempo and mood.

As the legato melodic line slowly unfolds over a richly colored accompaniment, it becomes clear that this is one of Felix's finest songs, anticipating the warmth and power of songs that Brahms wrote a generation later.

Literal Translation:

1) How gently the current moves, how quietly it carries the boat along. Far away are life and the place of my youth, far away is the pain that bound me there. Streams, carry me gently to the faraway land!

2) Overhead is the quiet home of the stars; below me is the river flowing on and on. Yes, you were rich, land of my youth. Truly what bound me there was sweet. Streams, carry me gently to the faraway land!

Scheidend

Original key: E major

"Voss" (Felix Mendelssohn)

Felix Mendelssohn
Opus 9, No. 6

Sehr ruhig

p   *cresc.*   *p*   *pp*

p tranquillo

(1.) Wie   so   ge - lin - - - de   die
(2.) Dro - ben   der   Ster - - - ne

Flut _____ be - wegt!   Wie   sie   so   ru - - hig   den
stil - - ler   Ort,   Wie   un - ten   der   Strom _____ fliesst

Na - - chen   trägt!   Fern _____ liegt   das   Le - ben,   das
fort _____ und   fort.   Wohl _____ warst   du   reich, _____ mein

SEHNSUCHT
[ze:nzʊxt]

(Longing)

fɛrn	ʊnt	fɛrnər	ʃalt	der	rɑ̯egən
1 Fern	**und**	**ferner**	**schallt**	**der**	**Reigen.**
Distant	and	more-distant	sounds	the	dance-tune.

vo:l	mi:r	ʊm	mɪç	he:r	ɪst ʃvɑ̯egən
2 Wohl	**mir!**	**um**	**mich**	**her**	**ist Schweigen**
Well	to-me!	Around	me	here	is silence

aof der flu:r
3 Auf der Flur;
on the land.

tsu:	dem	vɔllən	hɛrtsən	nu:r
4 Zu	**dem**	**vollen**	**Herzen**	**nur**
To	the	full	heart	only

vɪl	nɪçt	ru:	zɪç	nɑ̯egən
5 Will	**nicht**	**Ruh'**	**sich**	**neigen.**
will	not	rest	itself	bow.

hɔrç	di	naxt	ʃve:pt	dʊrç	di rɔ̯ømə
6 Horch!	**die**	**Nacht**	**schwebt**	**durch**	**die Räume.**
Hark!	the	night	soars	through	the spaces.

i:r	gəvant	dʊrçrɑ̯oʃt	di bɔ̯ømə
7 Ihr	**Gewand**	**durchrauscht**	**die Bäume**
Its	robe	through-rushes	the trees

lɪspəlnt lɑez
8 Lispelnd leis.
murmuring softly.

ax	zo:	ʃvɑ̯efən	li:bəhaes
9 Ach,	**so**	**schweifen**	**liebeheiß**
Ah,	thus	roam,	love-hot,

mɑenə	vynʃ	ʊnt	trɔ̯ømə
10 Meine	**Wünsch'**	**und**	**Träume.**
my	wishes	and	dreams.

Johann Gustav Droysen (1808–1884)

Poetic Background

"As the music fades away after the dance, the world grows quiet, but not my heart. The night seems filled with my wishes and dreams of love."

Please read about the poet in the notes to *Wartend*.

Line 1: *Reigen* is a round dance, in this case, the lively music for a round dance.

Line 2: *Wohl mir!* is untranslatable. English has an expression, "Woe is me!" but no correspondingly happy phrase, "Well is me!"

Interpretation

Within Opus 9, this song begins the second group, the *Das Mädchen* (The Girl). As in Felix's songs that precede it, the mood is intensely personal.

The singer is a young person who longs for love but does not yet know whom she loves. Fanny subtly symbolizes this uncertainty by opening the song with a chord that is not the tonic. The song remains on a subdued dynamic level throughout, but requires attention to the expression marks in both stanzas.

Sehnsucht

Johann Gustav Droysen

Fanny Hensel
Opus 9, No. 7

(1.) Fern _____ und fer - ner schallt der Rei - gen. Wohl
(2.) Horch! _____ die Nacht schwebt durch die Räu - me. Ihr Ge-

mir! um mich her _____ ist Schwei - gen _ auf der Flur; zu dem
wand durch - rauscht _ die Bäu - me _ lis - pelnd leis. Ach, so

vol - len Her - zen _ nur will nicht Ruh' _____ sich nei - gen,
schwei - fen lie - be - heiss mei - ne Wünsch' _____ und Träu - me,

will nicht Ruh' _____ sich _ nei - gen.
mei - ne Wünsch' _____ und _ Träu - me.

Literal Translation:

1) Farther and farther away fades the song of the dance. All is silent around me. Only in my full heart is there no peace yet.

2) Listen! night hovers in the sky. Her robe rustles softly through the trees.
Thus my passionate wishes and dreams roam the world.

FRÜHLINGSGLAUBE

[fryːlɪŋsglɑobə]

(Spring Faith)

	di	lɪndən	lʏftə	zɪnt	ɛrvɑxt
1	**Die**	**linden**	**Lüfte**	**sind**	**erwacht,**
	The	mild	breezes	have	awakened;

	ziː	zɔøzəln	ʊnt	veːbən	taːk	ʊnt	nɑxt
2	**Sie**	**säuseln**	**und**	**weben**	**Tag**	**und**	**Nacht,**
	they	whisper	and	weave	day	and	night;

	ziː	ʃɑfən	an	ɑllən	ɛndən
3	**Sie**	**schaffen**	**an**	**allen**	**Enden.**
	they	work	in	all	directions.

	oː	frɪʃər	dʊft	oː	nɔøər	klɑŋ
4	**O**	**frischer**	**Duft,**	**o**	**neuer**	**Klang!**
	O	fresh	fragrance,	o	new	sound!

	nuːn	ɑrməs	hɛrtsə	zae	nɪçt	baŋ
5	**Nun,**	**armes**	**Herze,**	**sei**	**nicht**	**bang!**
	Now,	poor	heart,	be	not	fearful!

	nuːn	mʊs	zɪç	ɑlləs	ɑlləs	vɛndən
6	**Nun**	**muß**	**sich**	**alles,**	**alles**	**wenden.**
	Now	must	itself	all,	all	turn.

	di	vɛlt	vɪrt	ʃøːnər	mɪt	jeːdəm	taːk
7	**Die**	**Welt**	**wird**	**schöner**	**mit**	**jedem**	**Tag,**
	The	world	becomes	lovelier	with	every	day;

	man	vaes	nɪçt	was	nɔx	veːrdən	maːk
8	**Man**	**weiß**	**nicht,**	**was**	**noch**	**werden**	**mag,**
	one	knows	not	what	yet	become	may.

	das	blyːən	vɪl	nɪçt	ɛndən
9	**Das**	**Blühen**	**will**	**nicht**	**enden.**
	The	blooming	will	not	end.

	nuːn	blyːt	das	fɛrnstə	tiːfstə	taːl
10	**Nun**	**blüht**	**das**	**fernste,**	**tiefste**	**Tal:**
	Now	blooms	the	farthest,	deepest	valley.

	nuːn	ɑrməs	hɛrts	fɛrgɪs	der	kvaːl
11	**Nun,**	**armes**	**Herz,**	**vergiß**	**der**	**Qual!**
	Now,	poor	heart,	forget	the	agony!

12 **Nun muß sich alles, alles wenden.**

Johann Ludwig Uhland (1787–1862)
[johɑn luːtvɪç uːlɑnt]

Poetic Background

"Spring brings hope and new possibilities. Even in my unhappy life, there has to be a change for the better."

Uhland was a Swabian poet but did not write in dialect. Felix met him later in life, but it is not known whether they had met before this song was composed. Like Felix, Uhland was called a classicist among the Romantics. Several of his poems are still widely sung in the manner of German folksongs.

Line 2: *weben* (weave) is a substitution for *wehen* (blow). Other poets have made the same substitution.

Line 10: *nun* (now) is Felix's word; Uhland wrote *Es blüht...* (In such a sentence, *es* has no meaning; it fills the place left vacant by moving the subject *Tal* to a position after the verb.)

Uhland dated his poem March 21, 1812, and it was published in 1813.

Interpretation

At first glance, this song resembles *Im Frühling,* but the mood now is quite different. The former song is full of longing and sighing; this one is jubilant. It also requires much quicker articulation of text. The dynamic markings, which reach both extremes, *pp* and *ff*, should be observed as closely as possible.

Stoner notes that this song anticipates the beginning of Felix's *Italian Symphony,* also in a quick 6/8 .

Schubert's *Frühlingsglaube,* D. 686, was published in Vienna in 1823; Felix probably was not familiar with it. In 1830 he knew *Erlkönig* and only a few other Schubert songs.

Frühlingsglaube

Johann Ludwig Uhland

Felix Mendelssohn
Opus 9, No. 8

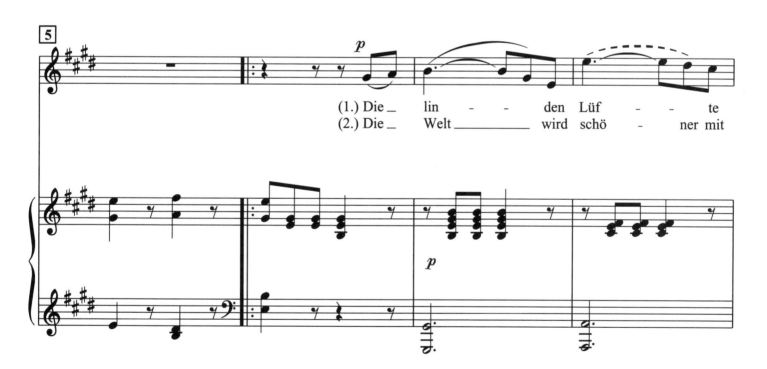

Literal Translation:

1) The mild breezes have begun to whisper and mingle day and night, working in all directions.
O fresh fragrance, new sound! Poor heart, now have no fear; everything will change!

2) The world grows more beautiful with every day; one does not know what may yet come of the endless blooming.
Even the farthest, deepest valley is in bloom. Poor heart, now forget your agony; everything will change!

den. O fri - scher Duft, o neu - er Klang! Nun muss sich, muss sich Al - les

den. Nun, ar - mes Herz, ver - giss_ der Qual! Nun muss sich, muss sich Al - les

wen - - den, nun muss _____ sich Al - les wen - -

wen - - den, nun muss _____ sich Al - les wen - -

den.

den.

FERNE
[fɛrnə]

(Distance)

ɪn vɑetə fɛrnə   vɪl ɪç trɔømən
1 **In weite Ferne   will ich träumen,**
Into wide distance want I   to-dream:

dɑː voː   duː vɑelst
2 **Da,   wo   du   weilst,**
there, where you stay,

voː   ɑos den ʃneːɪç   hɛllən rɔømən
3 **Wo   aus den schneeig hellen Räumen**
where from the snowy   bright spaces

di bɛçə ɪn di zeːən ʃɔømən
4 **Die Bäche in die Seen schäumen,**
the brooks into the lakes foam...

5 **Da, wo du weilst.**

vɪl   mɪt diːr durç di bɛrgə   ʃtrɑefən
6 **Will mit dir durch die Berge   streifen,**
I-want with you through the mountains to-roam,

7 **Da, wo du weilst.**

voː   ɑof dem ɑesfɛlt   gɛmzən ʃvɑefən
8 **Wo   auf dem Eisfeld Gemsen schweifen,**
where on the   ice-field chamois ramble,

ɪm   vɑrmən tɑːlə fɑegən rɑefən
9 **Im   warmen Tale Feigen reifen,**
in-the warm   valley figs   ripen...

10 **Da, wo du weilst.**

ʊnt hɑemlɪç vɪll ɪç vɑetər dəŋkən
11 **Und heimlich will ich weiter denken,**
And secretly will I   further think,

vɛn   duː hɑemkeːrst
12 **Wenn du heimkehrst,**
when you home-return.

ɛs mɑːk di tsɑet mɪç nɪçt bətryːbən
13 **Es mag die Zeit mich nicht betrüben,**
It may the time me   not   distress,

viːr zɪnt diːzɛlbən nɔx gəbliːbən
14 **Wir sind dieselben noch geblieben,**
We have the-same still   remained...

15 **Wenn du heimkehrst.**

Johann Gustav Droysen (1808–1884)

Poetic Background
"I dream about you on the mountains far away. And when you return home, may you find that we still love each other, unchanged."

Please read about Droysen in the notes to *Wartend*.

Line 3: *schneeig hellen Räumen* (snowy bright spaces) are spaces in the sense of open-air areas, mountain-tops, which are bright because of the year-round snow on them.

Line 4: *Die Bäche...schäumen* (the brooks...foam) because they fall turbulently down the mountainsides into the lakes.

Line 6: *Gemsen* (chamois) are hoofed, horned mammals that live in mountainous regions of Europe.

Line 7: *Feigen* (figs) do not ripen in any mountains in Germany, but perhaps in the valleys of the South Tirol, a German-speaking region that is now part of northern Italy.

Line 10: *Es* has no meaning in this sentence; it fills the place left vacant because the subject *Zeit*, which would normally precede the verb, is after the verb.

Interpretation
The tempo marking means "Lively, but gently." The basic beat is quick, but the sentiment is tender.

Notice the accent given to the word *du* (measures 3 and 11), which takes on as much feeling as if it were the beloved's name; that same expression must also be given to measures 15 and 23. In the third stanza, which begins in measure 24, the accompaniment is more richly harmonized and the vocal line is lifted higher for the last two phrases. The voice ending on the fifth scale degree symbolizes incompleteness, looking toward the future.

Ferne

Johann Gustav Droysen

Felix Mendelssohn
Opus 9, No. 9

In wei - te Fer - ne will ich träu - men, da, wo du weilst, wo aus den

schnee - ig hel - len Räu - men die Bä - che in die See - en schäu - men,

Literal Translation:

My dreams reach into the far distance, where you are, where from snowy, bright alpine fields the brooks ripple down to the lakes.

da, wo du weilst, da, wo du weilst. Will mit dir durch die Ber - ge

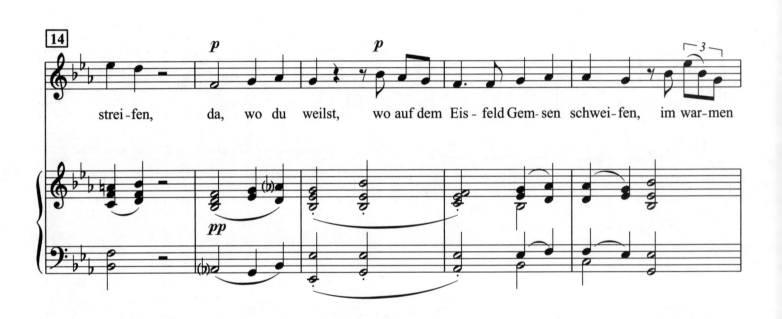

strei-fen, da, wo du weilst, wo auf dem Eis - feld Gem-sen schwei-fen, im war-men

Ta - le Fei - gen rei-fen, da, wo du weilst, da, wo du

I want to roam through the mountains, where you are, where chamois ramble on the glacier,
where figs ripen down in the warm valleys.

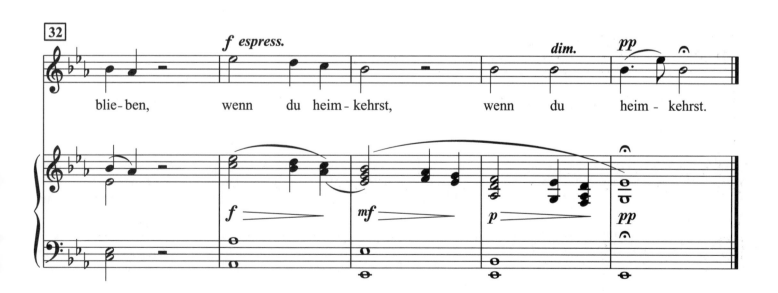

And secretly I think ahead to when you will come home. Time need not distress me;
we are still the same as we were, until you will come home.

VERLUST
[fɛrlʊst]

(Loss)

unt vʏstəns di bluːmən di klɑenən
1 Und wüßten's die Blumen, die kleinen,
And if-knew-it the flowers, the little-ones,

viː tiːf fɛrvʊndət mɑen hɛrts
2 Wie tief verwundet mein Herz,
how deeply wounded my heart,

ziː vʏrdən mɪt miːr vɑenən
3 Sie würden mit mir weinen,
they would with me weep

tsuː hɑelən mɑenən ʃmɛrts
4 Zu heilen meinen Schmerz.
to heal my pain.

unt vʏstəns di nɑxtɪgɑllən
5 Und wüßten's die Nachtigallen,
And if-knew-it the nightingales

viː ɪç zoː trɑorɪç ʊnt krank
6 Wie ich so traurig und krank,
how I so sad and sick,

ziː liːsən frøːlɪç ɛrʃallən
7 Sie ließen fröhlich erschallen
they would-let happily ring-out

ɛrkvɪkəndən gəzɑŋ
8 Erquickenden Gesang.
refreshing song.

unt vʏstən ziː mɑen veːə
9 Und wüßten sie mein Wehe,
And if-knew they my pain,

di gɔldnən ʃtɛrnəlɑen
10 Die goldnen Sternelein,
the golden little-stars,

ziː kɛːmən ɑos iːrər høːə
11 Sie kämen aus ihrer Höhe
they would-come from their height

unt ʃprɛːçən troːst miːr |aen
12 Und sprächen Trost mir ein.
and would-speak comfort to-me in.

diː |allə kœnnəns nɪçt vɪsən
13 Die alle können's nicht wissen,
They all can-it not know;

nuːr |aenər kɛnt mɑenən ʃmɛrts
14 Nur Einer kennt meinen Schmerz:
only one knows my pain.

er hat jaː zɛlpst tsɛrrɪsən
15 Er hat ja selbst zerrissen,
He has indeed himself torn-apart

tsɛrrɪsən miːr das hɛrts
16 Zerrissen mir das Herz.
torn-apart of-me the heart.

Heinrich Heine (1797–1856)
[hɑenrɪç hɑenə]

Poetic Background

"No one knows what pain my love has caused me!"

Heine's book *Tragedies* contains two verse plays separated by a *Lyrical Intermezzo,* which consists of 65 poems. These poems, written in 1822–23, tell about Heine's love for his cousin Amalie. She was the pretty daughter of a rich banker; Heine came from a poor family and was unsuccessful in business. When he went away to study, she promised to wait for him, but after two years she married a wealthy landowner.

Heine expressed his pain in short lyric poems. From the Berlin poet Wilhelm Müller, whose poems Schubert used for *Die schöne Müllerin* and *Winterreise,* Heine learned to write simple four-line stanzas that seem like folk songs. What was new in Heine's poems was an element of bitterness, often expressed in irony or sarcasm at the end.

While visiting Berlin, Heine had become an acquaintance of Fanny and Felix.

Line 14: Heine wrote the feminine form *Eine* (one woman), but Fanny changed it to the masculine *Einer* (one man). A female singer should use this text, but a male should use Heine's original words.

Line 15: Heine wrote *Sie* (she), but Fanny changed the pronoun to masculine.

Heine did not title his poems; the title must be Fanny's. Heine's poem has four four-line stanzas; Fanny combined them into two stanzas.

Interpretation

Although it begins quietly, the mood is agitated and builds quickly to a strong high note on *weinen* and an even stronger climax on *erquickenden.* The second stanza uses an interesting variation to heighten the expression of the words *kennt meinen Schmerz* (compare measures 13–14 with measures 33–34). The postlude conveys a feeling of incompleteness; there is no healing in this song.

This poem also appears in Schumann's great cycle *Dichterliebe* (Poet's Love, 1840). His song is gentler, more pleading than Fanny's; the implied anger emerges in the piano postlude.

Verlust

Heinrich Heine

Fanny Hensel
Opus 9, No. 10

Literal Translation:

And if the little flowers knew how deeply wounded my heart is, they would weep with me to heal my pain.

And if the nightingales knew how sad and sick I am, they would happily sing out their refreshing song.
And if the little stars knew my pain,

they would come down from the sky and comfort me. None of them can know; only one person knows my pain.
He himself tore my heart in pieces.

ENTSAGUNG
[ɛntzɑ̠ːɡʊŋ]

(Renunciation)

hɛr tsuː diːr vɪl ɪç mɪç rɛtən
1 **Herr, zu dir will ich mich retten,**
Lord, to you will I myself save

vɛn di vɛlt mɪç krɛŋkt ʊnt ʃlɛːkt
2 **Wenn die Welt mich kränkt und schlägt;**
when the world me offends and strikes;

vɪl ɪn dɑ̠enən ʃoːs mɪç bɛtən
3 **Will in deinen Schoß mich betten,**
will in your lap me bed,

vʊnt ʊnt myːd fɔn |ɑrɡən kɛtən
4 **Wund und müd' von argen Ketten,**
wounded and weary from heavy chains

di: mɑ̠enə ʃvaxə seːlə trɛːkt
5 **Die meine schwache Seele trägt.**
that my weak soul bears.

hɛr nax dɑ̠enər ɡnɑːd ʊnt trɔøə
6 **Herr, nach deiner Gnad' und Treue**
Lord, for your mercy and faithfulness

zeːnt zɪç mɑ̠en ɡə|ɛŋstɪçt hɛrts
7 **Sehnt sich mein geängstigt Herz,**
longs itself my fearful heart

das ɪç mɑ̠enə ʃʊlt bərɔøə
8 **Daß ich meine Schuld bereue,**
so-that I my guilt repent

das ɪç mɑ̠enən bʊnt ɛrnɔøə
9 **Daß ich meinen Bund erneue,**
so-that I my union renew,

fɔn jammər frae ʊnt frae fɔn ʃmɛrts
10 **Von Jammer frei und frei von Schmerz.**
from misery free and free from pain.

ɡɔt tsuː dɑ̠enəm zeːlɡən friːdən
11 **Gott, zu deinem sel'gen Frieden**
God, to your blessed peace

kɛːrət haem daen trɔøəs kɪnt
12 **Kehret heim dein treues Kind,**
returns home your faithful child,

diːr tsuː diːnən |oːn ɛrmyːdən
13 **Dir zu dienen ohn' Ermüden,**
you to serve without tiring,

dɪç tsuː ʃaoən froː bəʃiːdən
14 **Dich zu schauen froh beschieden,**
you to see happily summoned

voː mɪt diːr dɑ̠enə ɛŋəl zint
15 **Wo mit dir deine Engel sind.**
where with you your angels are.

Johann Gustav Droysen (1808–1884)

Poetic Background
"Lord, when the world is too hard for me, I trust that you will save me."

Please read about Droysen in the notes to *Wartend* .

Line 3: *Schoß* means, in a poetic sense, a place of refuge; in a literal sense, the lap or even the mother's body. Notice the long vowel. Two other words with the same spelling have the short vowel: *Schoß* (sprig); and *schoß*, past tense of *schießen* (to shoot).

Interpretation
Felix returns here to the mood of *Abendlied* and the comforting sweetness of the Biedermeier style (see the notes to *Abendlied*). When later generations rejected the Biedermeier aesthetic, critics also rejected this kind of music, calling it sentimental.

There is nonetheless much to admire in this music. The melody is unified by repeated use of a rising fourth in the first, second and fourth phrases, with a contrasting third phrase that moves only stepwise. After four two-measure phrases, the fifth phrase is extended to three measures and varied with a further extension to four measures. The accompaniment to the third stanza is strengthened in expression, primarily through artful attention to texture, which varies from empty octaves to chords of six notes.

If the six songs of *Das Mädchen* do intentionally form a story (see the preface), this song of Felix's is a bridge between two of Fanny's, making a transition from the despair of *Verlust* to the finality of *Die Nonne*.

Dynamics are given as they appear in the complete works, but they are confusing at measure 13, which has a diminuendo followed by a forte in measure 14. If one thinks of the forte as being on beat 3 of measure 13 (as the peak of the crescendo and diminuendo), all the other markings make sense.

Entsagung

Johann Gustav Droysen

Felix Mendelssohn
Opus 9, No. 11

Literal Translation:

1) Lord, I will flee to you when the world offends and mistreats me; I will find shelter in you when I am wounded and weary from the heavy chains that my weak soul bears.

2) Lord, my fearful heart longs for your mercy and your faithfulness, so much that I repent my misdeeds and renew my relationship with you, free from all misery and pain.

3) God, your faithful child returns home to your blessed peace, ready to serve you without tiring,
   summoned to see you in joy, where you are with your angels.

DIE NONNE

[di nɔnnə]

(The Nun)

ɪm   ʃtɪllən kloːstərgɑrtən
1 Im   stillen Klostergarten
In-the quiet   convent-garden

ɑenə blɑeçə junfrɑo gɪŋ
2 eine bleiche Jungfrau ging;
a   pale   maiden   walked.

der moːnt bəʃiːn   ziː tryːbə
3 Der Mond beschien sie trübe,
The moon lighted her dimly.

an iːrər vɪmpər hɪŋ
4 An ihrer Wimper hing
On her   eyelash hung

di trɛːnə tsɑrtər liːbə
5 Die Träne zarter   Liebe.
the tear   of-tender love.

oː voːl miːr das gəʃtɔrbən
6 "O wohl mir, daß gestorben
"O well to-me, that has-died

der trɔøə buːlə mɑen
7 Der treue Buhle mein!
the true   lover my.

ɪç darf   iːn viːdər liːbən
8 Ich darf   ihn wieder lieben:
I   am-allowed him again   to-love.

er vɪrt ɑen ɛŋəl zɑen
9 Er wird ein Engel sein,
He will an angel be,

ʊnt |ɛŋəl darf ɪç liːbən
10 Und Engel darf ich lieben."
and angels may I   love."

ziː trɑːt mɪt tsɑːgəm ʃrɪtə
11 Sie trat mit zagem   Schritte
She stepped with hesitant step

voːl tsum mariːɑbɪlt
12 Wohl zum Mariabild;
clear to-the Mary-picture.

ɛs ʃtɑnt ɪm lɪçtən ʃɑenə
13 Es stand im lichten Scheine,
It stood in bright light;

ɛs zɑː zoː mʊttermɪlt
14 Es sah so muttermild
it gazed, so mother-mild,

herʊntər ɑof di rɑenə
15 Herunter auf die Reine.
downward at   the pure-one.

ziː zɑnk tsuː zɑenən fyːsən
16 Sie sank zu seinen Füßen,
She sank at its   feet,

zɑː |ɑof mɪt hɪmməlsruː
17 Sah auf mit Himmelsruh,
looked up with heaven's-rest,

bɪs iːrə |ɑogənliːdər
18 Bis ihre Augenlider
until her eyelids

ɪm toːdə fiːlən tsuː
19 Im Tode fielen zu;
in death fell   shut;

iːr ʃlɑeər vɑltə niːdər
20 Ihr Schleier wallte nieder.
her veil   drifted down.

Johann Ludwig Uhland (1781–1826)

Poetic Background

"True love lasts forever, even beyond death."

Please read about Uhland in the notes to *Frühlingsglaube*. This love story in verse, written in 1805, has a sense of antiquity. Perhaps the young woman was sent to a convent by her family because she fell in love with a man they could not accept.

Line 8: *wieder* (again) implies that she loved a man before she became a nun, but as a nun she was forbidden to feel emotion for him.

Line 9: *Engel* (angel): that the soul of a dead person may become an angel is a common belief; it is not orthodox Christian teaching.

Interpretation

Recognizing the balladlike quality of the poem, Fanny gives it a strophic setting, but provides ample musical interest. Notice that *Der Mond beschien sie* is sung to the same melody as the beginning of the song but harmonized in a different key. The accompaniment moves constantly, like a gentle breeze blowing through the garden. Dynamics should vary between the stanzas, with the second stanza being the strongest and most personal in expression.

Die Nonne

Johann Ludwig Uhland

Fanny Hensel
Opus 9, No. 12

Literal Translation:

1) In the quiet convent garden a pale girl was walking. The moon shone dimly; on her eyelash hung a tear of love.

2) "I am happy that my true love has died! Now I may love him again, for he will be an angel, and I may love angels."

der Mond be - schien sie trü - - be, an ih - rer
Ich darf ihn wie - der lie - - ben: er wird ein

Wim - per hing die Trä - ne zar - ter Lie - - be.
En - gel sein, und En - gel darf ich lie - - ben."

(3.) Sie trat mit
(4.) Sie sank zu

3) She hesitantly approached the image of Mary; it shone and looked down maternally on the pure girl.

4) She sank down before the statue and gazed upward with heavenly peace until her eyes closed in death; her veil fluttered down.

THE SOUNDS OF GERMAN IN SINGING

German is usually the easiest foreign language for an English-speaking person to learn, because the two languages have common roots in the Germanic family of languages. It is enlightening to contrast them with two languages from the Romance family, French and Italian.

- *Nonlegato,* or frequent separation of sounds within a breath-phrase: Italian and French are highly legato. English and German are often nonlegato, although it is possible to create the illusion of legato in fine singing.

- *Syllabic stress:* In French all syllables except schwas have equal strength. Italian has stressed and unstressed syllables. English and German both have at least four levels of strength: primary and secondary stresses in multisyllabic words; unstressed syllables; and schwas, which are the weakest.

- *Vowel length:* German vowels are all clearly categorized as either short or long; precise time studies show that the distinction exists even in rapid speech. Italian also has long vowels before single consonants and short ones before double consonants. In French all vowels have equal length, except that at the end of a breath-phrase the last vowel (except for a schwa) is lengthened. In English the so-called long and short vowels differ in quality, but not necessarily in duration.

- *Consonant strength:* French and Italian consonant sounds are relatively gentle. English consonants are strong and expressive, and German is rich in forceful consonants.

- *Aspiration of plosives:* In French and Italian the plosive consonants [p], [t] and [k] are not aspirated. English and German plosives are spoken with aspiration (a puff of air that reinforces the consonant).

Characteristic German Sounds

Singers and actors use the standardized German pronunciation that is given in Siebs' *Deutsche Aussprache* (Berlin: de Gruyter, 1969). It should be noted that German vowels are more sharply defined and differentiated from each other than English vowels.

German has four mixed vowels not found in English, produced with the lips rounded while the tongue is simultaneously raised and moved forward. This combination of lip and tongue positions never occurs in English, and native English speakers must practice it for a time before it will feel natural.

Students quickly become aware of the two sounds of *ch* in German: the *ich* sound [ç], made with the mouth shaped for [ɪ]; and the *ach* sound [x], made with the mouth shaped for [ɑ]. Both *ch* sounds are made gently in singing, being just audible and never exaggerated. German natives may pronounce *ich* inconsistently so that it sometimes sounds like *isch,* but foreigners should avoid this.

The German language favors clarity over smoothness. Most words and syllables begin with consonants. A word or syllable that begins with a vowel is likely to be separated from whatever precedes it. Siebs refers to this as *Neueinsatz* (new onset). No firm rules determine when new onsets are needed. The IPA transcriptions in this book recommend a conservative minimum of them, indicated with [|].

Native German singers also differ as to the style of their onsets. The great baritone, Dietrich Fischer-Dieskau, consistently used soft onsets, while other singers sometimes use hard onsets or glottal stops.